D1357072

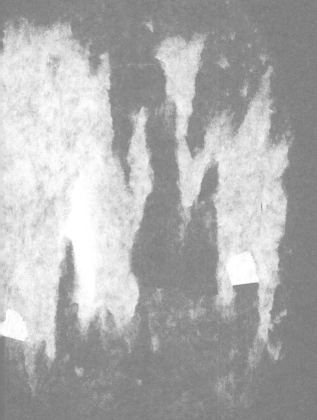

ALL THINGS SWEET

Rachel Allen

HarperCollins*Publishers*
77–85 Fulham Palace Road,
Hammersmith, London W6 8JB

www.harpercollins.co.uk

First published by HarperCollins*Publishers* 2014

A catalogue record of this book is available from the British Library.

ISBN: 978-0-00-746240-7

Food styling: Joss Herd
Prop styling: Tabitha Hawkins

Printed and bound in Italy by L.E.G.O. S.p.A.

ALL
THINGS
SWEET

Rachel Allen

**100 deliciously
sweet recipes
for every
occasion**

HarperCollins*Publishers*

Introduction

We all know about healthy eating and healthy lifestyles, and we all do our best to include wholesome food in our daily diets, but every now and then we deserve a treat, don't we?

In this book I've put together 100 delicious – and sometimes, admittedly quite decadent – recipes for sweet treats, from indulgent puddings, cooling ice creams and classic cakes to healthy sweet snacks and cookies for the kids.

The joy of baking and making your own treats is that you know exactly what has gone into them – so sometimes even the sweetest treat can be packed with nutritious and often healthy ingredients, such as fruit, seeds, nuts and yoghurt. I've tested all of these recipes and ensured that in lots of them the fresh and flavourful ingredients mean you can cut down on the sugar if you want to without sacrificing the taste.

In all the chapters I've tried to provide treats for every situation. The Quick treats chapter will give you just that – superfast steps to a sweet fix just when you need one. Fluffy blueberry pancakes or Yoghurt, toffee figs and honey are perfect breakfast bites to set you up for the day ahead or Quick cinnamon crumble cake or Superfast lemon ice cream will restore your senses after a long day. There's also a chapter of sweet things for children that you can whip up to reward the kids for great work – Crunchy, chewy ginger cookies with a glass of milk, Real fruit sugar popsicles on a hot summer's day, or Honey, cranberry and sesame oat bars for healthy but delicious lunch-box treats. Some of the recipes are so easy you can make them together with your children.

Sometimes I think fresh and fruity treats make me feel less guilty when I need to indulge my sweet tooth, simply by mixing sugary treats with healthy ingredients – Sweet labneh with honey, pistachios and orange blossom water brings a taste of the exotic, and refreshing and naughty Watermelon ginita always helps to cool down and unwind at the end of a hot day. And some days, when I'm rushed off my feet, I love a mini treat to keep me going, or something simple I can pack up for a picnic or pick at after dinner – Cinnamon cigars, Baklava and Pistachio, apricot and cardamom biscotti are all perfect restorative bites.

Of course, afternoon tea just calls out for sweet treats – what's tea without cake? Lavender sponge cake with rhubarb curd is perfect for a summer's day, or you could curl up in front of the fire with a piping hot cup of tea on a wet winter afternoon, munching on a delicious Pear and nutmeg cake.

When you're feeling really decadent or you want to impress, there are ridiculously rich and gooey recipes that will comfort and satisfy. When you're craving winter comfort food in summer, try a scoop of Apple crumble ice cream, or if you need a serious chocolate fix, bake an American chocolate fudge pie or a Double chocolate mousse cake. Showstoppers such as Layered mocha mousse coffee meringue, Chocolate coconut cake and Gooey date and stem ginger pudding will hit the spot and provide the wow factor for any dinner for friends.

And sometimes you just want the comfort of something you know well, so there's a whole chapter of classic recipes that have a little twist; favourite desserts get a fruity makeover in Blueberry bread and butter pudding and Apple and cinnamon baked cheesecake, and crème brulee gets a special salted caramel hit.

Personally I don't think you need a special occasion for a treat, but if you need an excuse, there is a chapter of puddings that will become festive favourites: Spiced plum tarte tatin or Nectarine and sloe gin jelly trifle for Christmas and New Year, or a Chocolate meringue cake for Easter.

So get over the guilt and make more of those 'me' moments, pick a treat and enjoy. With simple techniques, and lots of clever tips, there's something here for every mood and every situation. Make every day a special occasion.

Rachel Allen

Contents

QUICK

Roasted plums with white chocolate sauce

Quick cinnamon crumble cake

Fluffy blueberry pancakes with maple syrup

Really French toast!

Ivan's coconut and lime ice cream
with mango in mint syrup

Strawberry and rhubarb cobbler

Zesty fluffy orange pudding

Yoghurt, toffee figs and honey

Apricot and almond crumble

Superfast lemon ice cream

Strawberry, peach and vanilla fool
with orange sablé biscuits

Gooseberry clafoutis

A great little recipe this: simple, delicious and superfast, too. The white chocolate sauce will also feel very at home with fresh raspberries, blueberries, strawberries and blackberries.

Roasted plums with white chocolate sauce

SERVES 6

6 plums

6 tsp brown sugar

For the white chocolate sauce

100ml (3½fl oz) double or regular cream

25g (1oz) butter

100g (3½oz) white chocolate, chopped or in drops

Preheat the oven to 200°C (400°F), Gas mark 6.

Cut the plums in half, remove and discard the stones and lay the plums cut side up on a roasting tray. Scatter each half with ½ teaspoon of brown sugar and place in the oven to cook for 20–25 minutes or until the plums are tender and juicy.

To make the white chocolate sauce, place the cream and the butter in a saucepan and bring up to the boil to melt the butter. Take off the heat and add in the white chocolate, stirring to melt. Reheat the chocolate sauce just before serving.

To serve, drizzle warm plates generously with the warm white chocolate sauce and place the plums on top.

This cake, which has been inspired by German and Austrian baking, has become one of my go-to recipes for when I want something delicious to enjoy with a cup of coffee or tea.

Quick cinnamon crumble cake

SERVES 4–6

For the crumble

60g (2½oz) butter

100g (3½oz) brown sugar

1½ tsp ground cinnamon

50g (2oz) rolled (porridge) oats

For the cake

175g (6oz) plain flour

1 tsp baking powder

75g (3oz) caster sugar

½ tsp salt

75g (3oz) butter

1 egg

100ml (3½fl oz) milk

1 tsp vanilla extract

Equipment

20cm (8in) square tin

Preheat the oven to 180°C (350°F), Gas mark 4. Line the base and butter the sides of the tin.

Start by making the crumble top. Melt the butter and mix it in a bowl with the sugar, cinnamon and oats, then set aside.

Put all the dry ingredients for the cake mixture into the bowl of a food processor with the butter and buzz to make a crumbly texture. Mix together the egg, milk and vanilla extract and beat lightly, then pour into the flour and mix in the food processor, pulsing a couple of times until it forms a soft dough. Alternatively, place the flour, baking powder, sugar and salt in a bowl and rub in the butter, then mix in the beaten egg, milk and vanilla extract.

Pour the cake mixture into the lined tin and sprinkle the crumble topping over the top.

Place in the oven and bake for 25–30 minutes until set in the centre.

For a breakfast, brunch or mid-afternoon treat, these pancakes take just minutes to knock up and even less time to be demolished by your hungry ones!

Fluffy blueberry pancakes with maple syrup

MAKES ABOUT 12 PANCAKES

100g (3½oz) plain flour

25g (1oz) caster sugar

1 tsp baking powder

Pinch of salt

2 eggs, separated

125ml (4½fl oz) milk

2 tbsp sunflower oil

15g (½oz) butter

125g (4½oz) blueberries, fresh or frozen

To serve

Icing sugar

Maple syrup

Sift the flour, sugar, baking powder and salt into a bowl. In a separate bowl, mix together the egg yolks with the milk and whisk into the dry ingredients to form a thick batter. In another bowl, whisk the egg whites until stiff, then fold into the batter.

Place a frying pan on a medium–high heat. When the pan has heated up, drizzle over a few drops of sunflower oil and add a knob of butter to the pan. Allow to melt, then drop in three or four generous tablespoonfuls of batter at a time, leaving plenty of space in between.

Reduce the heat to medium–low, then place about seven blueberries on each pancake. After about 2 minutes, the pancakes should be turning golden underneath and holes should be forming on the top. At this stage, flip them over and cook for another 1–2 minutes until golden on both sides.

Serve the pancakes on a warm plate dusted with icing sugar and drizzled with maple syrup.

As if your average French toast weren't luxurious enough! When made with buttery croissants, this definitely has a certain *je ne sais quoi* about it. A great way of using up slightly stale croissants.

Really French toast!

SERVES 4

1 egg

2 tsp caster sugar

30ml (1¼fl oz) milk

½–1 tsp ground ginger

4 croissants, split in half lengthways

20g (¾oz) butter, for frying

Whisk together the egg, sugar, milk and ginger. Pour into a large, flat dish, place the croissants cut side down in the eggy mixture and allow to soak for a few minutes. Then turn to soak the other side.

Melt the butter in a frying pan over a medium heat. You will probably need to do this in two batches, so use half of the butter at a time. Fry the croissants cut side down first until golden brown, then flip over to cook the crusty side. Serve with a good drizzle of honey and maybe a dollop of softly whipped cream.

When my husband's cousin Ivan Whelan described this ice cream to me, I was instantly intrigued. Just three ingredients and, to top that, three of my very favourite ingredients. This ice cream delivers a rich, but extremely refreshing, punch of flavour. The mango in mint syrup, while not essential, does bring it all together to make a lovely way to end a meal.

Ivan's coconut and lime ice cream with mango in mint syrup

SERVES 6

For the ice cream

1 x 400g (14oz) tin of coconut milk

1 x 400g (14oz) tin of condensed milk

Juice and finely grated zest of 3 limes

For the mango in mint syrup

50g (2oz) caster or granulated sugar

20 mint leaves, finely chopped

Juice of ½ lime

1 large ripe mango, sliced

To make the ice cream, mix together all the ingredients well with a whisk, then pour into a container and place in the freezer for 3–4 hours until frozen.

In a small pan over a medium heat, dissolve the sugar in 50ml (2fl oz) water. Allow to cool slightly, then add the mint leaves and lime juice and mix the syrup with the mango slices.

Serve the ice cream with the slices of mango in the lime and mint syrup.

Strawberry and rhubarb has to be my favourite early-summer flavour combination and in this recipe, the two juicy fruits lie underneath a thick blanket of crunchy, buttery deliciousness.

Strawberry and rhubarb cobbler

SERVES 6

300g (11oz) rhubarb, cut into 2cm (¾in) pieces

300g (11oz) strawberries, sliced

100g (3½oz) caster sugar

For the batter

50g (2oz) butter, plus extra for greasing

225g (8oz) plain flour

2 tsp baking powder

75g (3oz) caster sugar

75ml (3fl oz) milk

1 egg

50g (2oz) almonds, chopped

25g (2oz) caster sugar

Equipment

1 litre (1¾ pint) capacity pie dish

Preheat the oven to 170°C (325°F), Gas mark 3.

Grease the pie dish with butter, then pour in the chopped rhubarb and strawberries and scatter over the caster sugar.

To make the batter, sift the flour and baking powder together into a bowl. Rub in the butter, then mix in 75g (3oz) of the sugar. Beat the milk and egg together and mix in to form a soft dough. Place in 'blobs' over the top of the fruit.

Mix the almonds together with the remaining sugar, then sprinkle over the top of the cobbler.

Place in the oven and bake for 45–50 minutes until the centre is cooked through. Stick a skewer into the batter – the cobbler is ready if it comes out clean.

A firm family favourite in our house. This is the kind of pudding I love after something cosy like roast chicken, mashed potatoes and lashings of gravy.

Zesty fluffy orange pudding

SERVES 4

25g (1oz) butter

250g (9oz) caster or granulated sugar

2 eggs, separated

25g (1oz) plain flour

Zest and juice of 1 orange

Juice of ½ lemon

150ml (5fl oz) milk

Equipment

1 litre (1¾ pint) capacity ovenproof dish

Preheat the oven to 180°C (350°F), Gas mark 4.

Place the butter, sugar and egg yolks in a bowl and cream together, using a wooden spoon or the paddle attachment of an electric food mixer, until light and fluffy.

Sift in the flour, then fold into the mixture along with the orange zest, orange and lemon juice, and milk.

In a separate, clean dry bowl, whisk together the egg whites until they form stiff peaks. Fold the egg whites into the orange mixture.

Pour the mixture into the dish, then place in the oven and bake for about 40 minutes. The top should be set, with a layer of orange curd on the bottom. Remove from the oven and serve with softly whipped cream or ice cream.

Something magical happens when figs are cooked with brown sugar. As the sugar caramelises, the figs take on a flavour like that of a sweet, dark, toffee-like sherry. The tangy Greek yoghurt is the perfect foil for the figs – and when toasted pine nuts and a drizzle of honey are added into the mix, this makes for a delightful Middle-Eastern-inspired treat.

Yoghurt, toffee figs and honey

SERVES 4

20g (¾oz) soft light brown sugar

4–8 ripe figs, depending on size

300g (11oz) Greek yoghurt

4 tsp honey

25g (1oz) pine nuts, toasted (see tip below)

Spread the sugar out on a plate, then cut the figs in half.

Place a frying pan on a medium–high heat. Place the figs cut side down in the sugar, then place in the frying pan. Cook for a few minutes until the sugar darkens and caramelises.

As the figs cook, divide the yoghurt among the plates, drizzle over the honey and sprinkle with the toasted pine nuts. Arrange the figs on the plate next to the yoghurt, then serve.

Rachel's Tip: To toast the pine nuts, place in a non-stick pan over a medium–high heat and cook for a minute or so, tossing once or twice, until slightly darker in colour and toasted.

Have you ever split open an apricot stone and eaten the little almond-like kernel inside? I did when I was really young and I still remember its bitter but very almondy flavour. This is why apricot kernels feature in many almond-flavoured delicacies, such as amaretto and amaretti biscuits. Anything made with apricots goes with almonds – and vice versa. This crumble is a lovely take on an age-old pairing of ingredients.

Apricot and almond crumble

SERVES 6

10 ripe apricots (650g/1lb 7oz in weight, with stones)

75g (3oz) caster sugar

For the crumble

150g (5oz) plain flour

100g (3½oz) caster sugar

75g (3oz) butter, cubed

50g (2oz) whole almonds with their skins on, roughly chopped

Equipment

1 litre (1¾ pint) capacity pie dish

Preheat the oven to 180°C (350°F), Gas mark 4.

Cut the apricots in half, then remove the stones and cut each half in half again. Place these apricot quarters in the pie dish and sprinkle with the caster sugar, then set aside while you make the crumble.

Place the flour and the sugar in a bowl and rub in the butter to resemble coarse breadcrumbs. Stir in the almonds, then scatter the crumble over the fruit to cover.

Bake in the oven for 20–30 minutes until the crumble is golden, bubbling and the fruit is deliciously tender.

Serve with softly whipped cream or ice cream.

We've always known that opposites attract. Here's a perfect example: smooth, rich, velvety cream and sharp, refreshing, tangy lemon couldn't be more different, but with just some sugar to bring them together, they're a match made in heaven.

Superfast lemon ice cream

SERVES 4

2 lemons

150g (5oz) caster sugar

300ml (½ pint) double or regular cream

First, finely grate the zest from one of the lemons, then squeeze the juice from both. Strain the juice into the zest and add the sugar, stirring and gradually adding the cream. It will thicken slightly as you add it. Pour it into a container and place in the freezer.

Freeze until solid around the outside and mushy in the centre. Mix with a fork and place back in the freezer again to freeze until firm.

I used to assume that a fruit fool was called a fool because any fool could make it (try to say that really quickly ten times!), but the term actually comes from the French verb *fouler*, which means 'to crush'. This is a gorgeous way to end a summer feast.

Strawberry, peach and vanilla fool with orange sablé biscuits

SERVES 6–8

For the orange sablé biscuits

Makes 40–45

150g (5oz) butter, softened

110g (4oz) caster sugar

1 egg

Finely grated zest of 1 orange

275g (10oz) plain flour

½ tsp baking powder

For the fool

225g (8oz) strawberries

2 ripe peaches, halved and stones removed

125g (4½oz) caster sugar

2 tsp vanilla extract

Juice of 1 lemon

2 egg whites

150ml (5fl oz) double or regular cream

First make the biscuits. Place the butter in a bowl and beat until soft. Add in the sugar and beat again until light and creamy. Add in the egg and the orange zest, then sift in the flour and the baking powder and mix to bring together.

Place the dough on a sheet of baking parchment and roll into a log about 35cm (14in) long and 5cm (2in) in diameter. Cover with the baking parchment and twist at the ends to close. This can sit in the fridge for 2 weeks or it can be frozen for up to 3 months.

When ready to cook, preheat the oven to 180°C (350°F), Gas mark 4.

Cut the dough into slices 5–7.5mm (about ¼in) thick. Place on a baking tray lined with baking parchment and bake for 8–12 minutes until light golden. Take out of the oven and let sit for 2–3 minutes before transferring to a wire rack to cool.

Place the strawberries, peaches, 75g (3oz) of the sugar, vanilla extract and lemon juice in a blender and whiz up, then push through a sieve into a bowl.

In another bowl, whisk the egg whites with the remaining sugar until stiff peaks appear. Then whisk the cream until almost, but not quite, stiffly whipped. Fold the egg-white mixture into the fruit, then gently fold in the whipped cream until light and fluffy.

Serve with the orange sablé biscuits.

Rachel's Tip: This mixture freezes well to make an ice cream.

While most traditional clafoutis recipes contain cherries, I find that gooseberries make a delicious alternative. The sharp, tangy flavour of the berries is perfectly complemented by the sweet vanilla custard. I adore eating this still a little warm from the oven, with cold, softly whipped cream.

Gooseberry clafoutis

SERVES 4–6

25g (1oz) butter

350g (12oz) gooseberries (fresh or frozen), topped, tailed and cut in half

125g (4½oz) brown sugar

2 tbsp brown sugar, for sprinkling

For the batter

125ml (4½fl oz) milk

125ml (4½fl oz) double or regular cream

4 eggs

60g (2½oz) plain flour

100g (3½oz) caster sugar

1 tsp vanilla extract

Equipment

1 litre (1¾ pint) capacity pie dish

Preheat the oven to 180°C (350°F), Gas mark 4 and place the pie dish in the oven to heat up.

Place a frying pan on a high heat. Tip in the butter, gooseberries and the brown sugar. Cook, uncovered, for about 5–8 minutes, until the gooseberries have softened and sweetened.

While this cooks, place all the ingredients for the batter in a blender or food processor (or just a bowl using a hand whisk) and whiz/whisk until completely blended.

Take the dish out of the oven, pour the gooseberries and all their juices into the dish, then pour the batter over the gooseberries carefully so as not to disturb the fruits. Scatter the 2 tablespoons of brown sugar over the top and cook in the oven for 40 minutes or until a skewer inserted into the centre comes out clean.

SWEET THINGS FOR CHILDREN

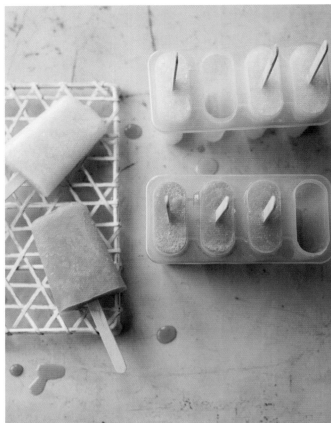

Banoffee ice cream

Milk chocolate mousse, caramel sauce,
toffee popcorn

Chocolate peanut brittle butter cookies

Crunchy, chewy ginger cookies

Rocky Road bites

Tropical fruit sorbet

Choux nuts with cinnamon sugar and
pastry cream

Deep-fried honey puffs

Melon popsicles

Warm chocolate spoon cake

Cinnamon and maple oat cookies

Dulce de leche brownies

Peanut butter and chocolate ripple ice cream

Honey, cranberry and sesame oat bars

Taking its name from the ubiquitous Banoffee Pie, which has a biscuit base topped with banana slices, toffee (or boiled condensed milk) and heaps of whipped cream, this ice cream is always a winner with children. Delicious vanilla ice cream with ripples of boiled condensed milk, crunchy biscuits and caramelised bananas; too good not to be shared with the adults!

Banoffee ice cream

SERVES 8–10

For the banoffee

1 x 400g (14oz) tin of full-fat condensed milk

75g (3oz) butter

75g (3oz) caster or granulated sugar

4 bananas, cut in quarters lengthways, then sliced

12 digestive biscuits, broken into pieces

For the ice cream

4 egg yolks

100g (3½oz) caster or granulated sugar

1 tsp vanilla extract

1.2 litres (2 pints) softly whipped cream (measured when whisked)

Boil the unopened tin of condensed milk in a large saucepan for 2½ hours, topping up the water from time to time, then remove from the heat and allow the tin to cool in the water.

To make the ice cream, place the egg yolks in a bowl and whisk until light and fluffy. Combine the sugar and 250ml (9fl oz) water in a small saucepan, then stir over a medium heat until the sugar is completely dissolved. Remove the spoon and boil the syrup until it reaches the 'thread' stage, 106–113°C (223–235°F). It will look thick and syrupy and when a metal spoon is dipped in, the last drops of syrup will form thin threads. Pour this boiling syrup in a steady stream onto the egg yolks, whisking all the time. Add the vanilla extract and continue to whisk until it becomes a thick, creamy white mousse. Fold in the softly whipped cream, place in a container, cover and place in the freezer for an hour.

Place the butter and sugar in a pan on a medium heat. When the butter has melted, add the bananas and continue to bubble for a few minutes until the sugar browns and caramelises. Then remove from the heat and allow to cool.

Remove the ice cream from the freezer, fold in the broken biscuits and toffee bananas, then add the boiled condensed milk in ½ teaspoon amounts, continuing to mix and fold.

Return to the freezer and allow to freeze for about 3–4 hours until frozen all through.

Rachel's Tip: Do not use 'light' condensed milk, as it will not set on boiling.

Popcorn never fails to add a playful, Willy Wonka-like note to a dish. But it's more than just a bit of fun here, as it adds a welcome crunch with the slightest hint of salt to the sweet chocolate mousse and caramel sauce. This is a great assemble-it-yourself recipe for children.

Milk chocolate mousse, caramel sauce, toffee popcorn

Serves 4–6

For the chocolate mousse

125g (4½oz) milk chocolate

75ml (3fl oz) double or regular cream

2 eggs, separated

For the toffee popcorn

1 tbsp sunflower oil

25g (1oz) popcorn kernels

20g (¾oz) butter

Pinch of salt

20g (¾oz) brown sugar

1 tbsp golden syrup

Cont. opposite

Finely chop the chocolate. In a saucepan, bring the cream up to the boil, turn off the heat, add the chocolate to the cream and stir it around until the chocolate melts. Allow to cool slightly, then whisk in the egg yolks.

In a separate clean, dry bowl, whisk the egg whites until just stiff, then stir a quarter of the egg white into the cream mixture. Gently fold the chocolate mixture into the rest of the egg whites.

Spoon into little bowls, glasses or cups or one serving bowl and leave in the fridge for 2–3 hours to set.

Next make the toffee popcorn. Place the oil in a saucepan with a lid on a medium–low heat. Add the popcorn kernels and swirl the pan to coat the popcorn in the oil. Put the lid on, then turn the heat down to low and listen for the popping! As soon as the popping stops, turn off the heat and tip into a bowl.

Melt the butter in a separate saucepan with the pinch of salt, add the brown sugar and golden syrup and stir over a high heat for 1–2 minutes. Pour the toffee over the popcorn, and toss to mix in the toffee sauce. Allow to cool.

As it cools, the toffee surrounding the popcorn will harden – break it up with your hands so that it doesn't set into one great big lump.

For the caramel sauce

225g (8oz) caster or
granulated sugar

110g (4oz) butter

175ml (6fl oz) double or
regular cream

To make the caramel sauce, dissolve the sugar in 75ml (3fl oz) water in a pan over a medium heat. Stir in the butter, raise the heat a little and bubble, stirring occasionally, until it turns a light toffee colour. This may take about 15–20 minutes. Turn off the heat and stir in half the cream. When the bubbles die down, stir in the rest of the cream.

The sauce can be stored in the fridge for up to 2 weeks and reheated when necessary.

To serve, drizzle the caramel sauce over the chocolate mousse, then scatter with the toffee popcorn.

Simple shortbread biscuits dipped in melted milk chocolate, then scattered with salted peanut brittle; this could be the perfect cookie.

Chocolate peanut brittle butter cookies

MAKES 20 COOKIES

For the peanut brittle

40g (1½oz) caster or granulated sugar

40g (1½oz) salted peanuts

For the cookies

150g (5oz) plain flour

50g (2oz) caster or granulated sugar

100g (3½oz) butter, softened

To finish

100g (3½oz) milk chocolate, in drops or broken into pieces

To make the peanut brittle, first line a baking tray with baking parchment and set aside. Place the sugar in a frying pan and scatter the peanuts over the sugar. Place on a medium heat, not stirring but swirling the pan every so often to caramelise the sugar evenly. Cook until the sugar has completely melted and is a deep golden colour. Swirl the pan again so that the peanuts are coated in the caramel. Transfer the coated nuts to the prepared baking tray. Once cool and completely set (it will be hard), break up the brittle using your hands, then place in a food processor and whiz until just slightly coarse or chop coarsely by hand.

Preheat the oven to 180°C (350°F), Gas mark 4. Put the flour and sugar into a mixing bowl. Rub in the soft butter and bring the whole mixture together to form a stiff dough. Alternatively, you can whiz everything up briefly in a food processor. Roll the dough into a log approximately 30cm (12in) long and 4cm (1½in) in diameter (the log of cookie dough can be covered and kept in the fridge like this for up to a week). Now cut into 7mm (¼in) slices.

Place on baking trays (no need to butter or line) and cook in the oven for 8–10 minutes until light golden brown. Allow to cool for 1 minute before placing on a wire rack to cool completely.

Alternatively, you could roll out the dough to about 7mm (¼in) thick and cut it into shapes to bake.

Once the cookies have cooled, place the chocolate in a bowl sitting over a saucepan with a few centimetres of water. Bring the water up to the boil, then take off the heat and allow the chocolate to melt slowly. Once melted, dip the top of each cookie into the chocolate, then scatter the peanut brittle over the chocolate and place somewhere cool to set.

I love how, when cookies have golden syrup in them, they manage to be both crunchy and chewy at the same time. Packed with ground ginger and cinnamon, these cookies are great for a snack with a glass of cold milk.

Crunchy, chewy ginger cookies

MAKES 18–20 COOKIES

125g (4½oz) butter

75g (3oz) brown sugar

75g (3oz) golden syrup

1 egg, beaten

150g (5oz) plain flour

1 tsp bicarbonate of soda

3 tsp ground ginger

1½ tsp ground cinnamon

1½ tsp mixed spice

50g (2oz) caster or granulated sugar

Beat the butter, then add in the brown sugar, the golden syrup and then the egg. Use a whisk for a few seconds to bring the mixture together. Take out the whisk, then sift in the remaining ingredients, but not the sugar.

The mixture can be used straight away or it can placed in the fridge for 1 week.

Preheat the oven to 180°C (350°F), Gas mark 4. Line a baking tray with baking parchment.

Place the sugar in a bowl. Take dessertspoonfuls of the cookie dough, roll into balls, toss in the sugar, flatten and place spaced apart on the lined tray.

Bake for 12–15 minutes until just set, but still slightly soft in the centre. Take out of the oven and let sit for 4 minutes before removing to a wire rack to cool.

This particular Rocky Road recipe is a bit of a homage to the Daim bar. Originally known as Dajm in Swedish, we in Ireland and the UK first knew of it as a Dime bar. I remember when they first came out in Ireland; I immediately adored the brittle toffee with bits of almond, all covered in milky chocolate. Anyway, when chopped up with marshmallows and biscuits before being stirred into melted chocolate and golden syrup and allowed to set, this is a Rocky Road that I love to take.

Rocky Road bites

MAKES ABOUT
25 SQUARES

450g (1lb) milk or dark chocolate (55–70% cocoa solids) or ½ of each

75g (3oz) golden syrup

4 x 28g (1¼oz) Daim bars, broken into chunks

150g (5oz) marshmallows, chopped

200g (7oz) biscuits, such as shortbread, leftover cookies or digestives, broken into chunks

Equipment

20cm (8in) square tin

Line the tin with baking parchment on the base and up the sides.

Melt the chocolate with the golden syrup, then remove from the heat. Add in the remaining ingredients, then press into the tin. Place somewhere cool for a couple of hours to set.

Cut into squares to serve.

The day that I tested this recipe at home I happened to have half a dozen or so children at our house. This sorbet disappeared in front of my very eyes. The banana adds a smooth sweetness to the pineapple, giving you that totally tropical taste.

Tropical fruit sorbet

SERVES 6

1 medium banana

½ pineapple, peeled and cored (about 200g/7oz)

Juice of 1 large orange (about 150ml/5fl oz)

Juice of 1 large lime (about 50ml/½fl oz)

100g (3½oz) caster or granulated sugar

Equipment

Ice-cream machine (optional)

Place all the ingredients in a food processor and whiz together until smooth. Taste for sweetness – you're looking for a balance between sweet and sharp. Add more lime juice or sugar to get the right balance if necessary.

Freeze in an ice-cream machine according to the manufacturer's instructions. Alternatively, put in a container in the freezer and leave for an hour. Remove from the freezer and whisk, then return to the freezer. Repeat this process two or three more times.

OK, these are most definitely not an everyday treat, but it has to be said they are completely divine. Like doughnuts, but made with the faster-to-put-together choux pastry, these will disappear as soon as they're made.

Choux nuts with cinnamon sugar and pastry cream

SERVES 8–10

For the choux pastry

100g (3½oz) strong white or plain flour

Pinch of salt

75g (3oz) butter

3 eggs, beaten

Sunflower or vegetable oil, for deep-frying

For the pastry cream

4 egg yolks

100g (3½oz) caster sugar

25g (1oz) plain flour, sifted

1 vanilla pod, with a line scored down the side, or ½ tsp vanilla extract

350ml (12fl oz) milk

For the cinnamon sugar

50g (2oz) caster or granulated sugar

1 tsp ground cinnamon

First, make the choux pastry. Sift the flour and salt into a large bowl and set aside.

Place 150ml (5fl oz) water and the butter in a medium-sized saucepan with high sides, set over a medium-high heat and stir until the butter melts. Allow the mixture to come to a rolling boil, then immediately remove the pan from the heat. Add the flour and salt and beat in very well with a wooden spoon until the mixture comes together.

Reduce the heat to medium and return the saucepan to the heat, stirring for 1 minute until the mixture starts to 'fur' (slightly stick to the base of the pan). Remove from the heat and allow to cool for 1 minute.

Pour about a quarter of the beaten egg into the pan and, using the wooden spoon, beat very well. Add a little more egg and beat well again until the mixture comes back together. Continue to add the egg, beating vigorously all the time, until the mixture has softened, is nice and shiny and has a dropping consistency. You may not need to add all the egg or you may need a little extra. If the mixture is too stiff (not enough egg), then the choux pastries will be too heavy, but if the mixture is too wet (too much egg), they will not hold their shape when spooned onto greaseproof paper.

Although the pastry is best used right away, it can be placed in a bowl, covered and chilled for up to 24 hours, until ready to use.

Cont. overleaf

Next, make the pastry cream. In a bowl, whisk the egg yolks with the sugar until light and thick, then stir in the flour.

Place the vanilla pod, if using, in a saucepan with the milk and bring it slowly just up to the boil. Remove the vanilla pod and pour the milk onto the egg yolk mixture, whisking all the time. Return the mixture to the pan and stir over a low–medium heat until it comes up to a gentle boil (it must boil for it to thicken). Continue to cook, stirring all the time (or use a whisk if it looks lumpy), for 2 minutes or until it has thickened. The mixture is thick enough when it falls off the spoon in large blobs rather than pouring off it. If the mixture goes a little lumpy while cooking, remove the saucepan from the heat and whisk well.

After 2 minutes, remove the saucepan from the heat, add the vanilla extract, if using, and pour into a bowl. If it is still lumpy now cooked, push it through a sieve.

Cover with cling film and allow to cool. It must be covered or the surface must be rubbed with a tiny knob of butter to prevent a skin from forming.

To make the cinnamon sugar, combine the sugar and cinnamon and set aside.

When you're ready to cook the choux nuts, turn on a deep fryer to 180°C (350°F), or place the oil in a saucepan on a medium–high heat. The oil is ready to cook with when a small piece of bread dropped into it bubbles and rises quickly back up to the surface.

Scoop up little blobs of the choux pastry with a kitchen teaspoon, round and scoop off with a second teaspoon, drop into the deep-fat fryer and fry for 5–6 minutes, turning over a few times, until they are four times the size and golden brown.

Remove, drain briefly on kitchen paper, and then, using a skewer or the tip of a small sharp knife, make a hole in the side or the base of each puff. Toss the puffs in the cinnamon sugar, then, using a small piping bag and small nozzle, pipe pastry cream into the centre through the hole you have just made. Serve while warm.

Little puffs of honey deliciousness, these are best eaten while still warm. That won't be a problem at all, but make sure to save some for yourself.

Deep-fried honey puffs

MAKES ABOUT
20 PUFFS

350ml (12fl oz) water, at blood temperature

2 tbsp honey

10g (⅜oz) dried yeast or 20g (¾oz) fresh yeast

300g (11oz) plain flour

25g (1oz) cornflour

½ tsp salt

Sunflower or vegetable oil, for deep-frying

To serve

100ml (3½fl oz) honey

Icing sugar, for dusting

Place the water in a bowl or jug and stir in the honey to mix. Add in the yeast and leave to stand on your worktop for 5 minutes. Meanwhile, mix together in a bowl the flour, cornflour and salt.

Pour the yeast and honey water into the dry ingredients and stir well to mix. Cover with cling film and leave to stand at room temperature for 30 minutes until bubbles start to appear on the surface. The puff batter can also be placed in the fridge, where it will sit perfectly for up to 24 hours.

When you are ready to cook the puffs, turn on a deep fryer to 180°C (350°F), or place the oil (a tasteless oil such as sunflower or vegetable oil) in a saucepan on a medium–high heat. The oil is ready to cook with when a small piece of bread dropped into it bubbles and rises quickly back up to the surface. While you're waiting for the oil to heat up, place some kitchen towel on a baking tray or a wide bowl.

Using a dessertspoon, scoop out a spoonful of the batter and, using another dessertspoon, scrape it off into the oil. Put a few more spoonfuls into the oil, but don't overcrowd it or the temperature will drop, resulting in oily, heavy puffs. I like to cook about six at a time. Allow them to cook for about 2 minutes until golden on the bottom, then tip over and cook on the other side for about 2 minutes or until golden again.

When cooked, the puffs will be golden all over and cooked through in the centre. Using a slotted spoon, lift the puffs out of the oil and onto the kitchen towel to drain.

Serve warm with a dusting of icing sugar, a drizzle of honey over the top and a scoop of ice cream on the side, if you wish.

Rachel's Tip: I sometimes scatter chopped toasted nuts such as walnuts, pistachios or hazelnuts over the honey when serving these.

A popsicle is a great refreshing treat to serve after a meal or just any time on a sunny day, and when made with sweet, ripe melons, hardly any sugar is needed. The children might not want to share these with you.

Melon popsicles

**MAKES 8 X 50ML
(2FL OZ) POPSICLES**

400g (14oz) honeydew, cantaloupe or Galia melon flesh (about ¼ melon with the seeds and skin removed)

40ml (1½fl oz) lemon juice (about ½ lemon)

40g (1½oz) caster sugar (if you use a Galia melon, you might need more sugar)

Equipment

Ice lolly/popsicle moulds

Put the melon flesh, lemon juice and sugar in a blender and whiz until completely smooth. Pour into the popsicle moulds and place in the freezer for 4–6 hours until frozen.

Rachel's Tip: Other summer fruits also work well in these popsicles. Try using peaches, raspberries or strawberries.

Not quite a cake, not quite a pudding, this gluten-free recipe has lots of ground almonds in it to keep it deliciously nutty and fudgy.

Warm chocolate spoon cake

SERVES 4–6

150g (5oz) dark chocolate (55–70% cocoa solids)

150g (5oz) butter

125g (4½oz) caster sugar

1 tsp vanilla extract

75g (3oz) ground almonds

4 eggs, separated

Pinch of salt

Equipment

1 litre (1¾ pint) capacity pie dish

Preheat the oven to 190°C (375°F), Gas mark 5.

Place the chocolate, butter and sugar in a bowl sitting over a saucepan of simmering water and allow to melt. Take the bowl off the heat and stir in the vanilla extract, the ground almonds and the four egg yolks, one by one.

Put the egg whites in a bowl with the pinch of salt and whisk just until stiff, but still creamy rather than grainy.

Fold in the chocolate mixture and tip into the pie dish.

Bake in the oven for 22–25 minutes until the outsides are set and the centre just has a thick wobble. If you take this out of the oven before it has completely cooked, it will stay nutty and fudgy, even when it cools down.

Allow to sit for a few minutes before serving. Wonderful with cold, softly whipped cream or ice cream.

One taste of cinnamon mixed with maple syrup never fails to take me back to family holidays visiting our relatives in Canada. I was so enthralled with this classic North American flavour that I find myself using it time and time again in baking.

Cinnamon and maple oat cookies

MAKES 24 COOKIES

100g (3½oz) butter

100ml (3½fl oz) maple syrup

125g (4½oz) plain flour

¼ tsp bicarbonate of soda

125g (4½oz) caster sugar

1½ tsp ground cinnamon

150g (5oz) rolled (porridge) oats

1 egg

Preheat the oven to 180°C (350°F), Gas mark 4.

Place the butter and maple syrup in a saucepan on a medium heat and stir together until the butter has melted. Then set aside and allow to cool slightly.

Sift the flour and bicarbonate of soda into a mixing bowl, then stir in the sugar, cinnamon and oats. Mix the egg with the butter and maple syrup and then mix with the dry ingredients to form a soft, sticky dough.

Spoon out the mixture onto a lined baking tray using two dessertspoons, forming balls of dough spaced at least 2–3cm (1in) apart.

Bake in the oven for about 15 minutes until spread out and just dry to the touch. Once out of the oven, allow the cookies to sit on the tray for a few minutes to set before transferring to a wire rack to cool.

As if brownies aren't good enough already, these are outrageously divine, with ripples of boiled condensed milk swirling through dense chocolate heaven.

Dulce de leche brownies

MAKES 16 SQUARES

½ x 400g (14oz) tin of full-fat condensed milk or ½ x 400g (14oz) tin of dulce de leche (also labelled 'caramel')

175g (6oz) dark chocolate (55–70% cocoa solids)

175g (6oz) butter, cubed

25g (1oz) good-quality cocoa powder, sifted

3 eggs

225g (8oz) caster or soft light brown sugar

1 tsp vanilla extract

100g (3½oz) plain flour

Equipment

20cm (8in) square cake tin

Boil the unopened tin of condensed milk in a large saucepan for 2½ hours, topping up the water from time to time, then remove from the heat and allow the tin to cool in the water.

Preheat the oven to 180°C (350°F), Gas mark 4. Line the base and sides of the cake tin with baking parchment.

Melt the chocolate, butter and cocoa powder together in a bowl set over a saucepan with a few centimetres of simmering water. Do not let the base of the bowl touch the water. Remove from the heat.

In a separate large bowl, whisk the eggs, sugar and vanilla extract for 2 minutes until a little light and creamy. Continuing to whisk, add the chocolate mixture until well combined. Sift in the flour and fold through with a spatula or metal spoon.

Spoon the mixture into the prepared tin. Use a teaspoon to add blobs of the boiled condensed milk/dulce de leche/caramel all over the surface of the brownies. Then using a small sharp knife or skewer, run it around in swirls for a marbled effect.

Bake in the oven for 20–25 minutes. When cooked it should be dry on top, but still slightly 'gooey' and 'fudgy' inside. Don't be tempted to leave it in the oven any longer than this or you will have cake and not brownies. Allow to cool in the tin, then cut into squares.

Rachel's Tip: Do not use 'light' condensed milk, as it will not set on boiling.

No wonder so many different chocolate bars contain both peanut butter and chocolate; it's a winning combination, and particularly so in this ice cream. All you need now is a good movie and a spoon.

Peanut butter and chocolate ripple ice cream

SERVES 6-8

30ml (1fl oz) water

30ml (1oz) caster sugar

50g (2oz) dark chocolate

75g (3oz) crunchy peanut butter

2 eggs

100g (3½oz) caster or granulated sugar

1 tsp vanilla extract

250ml (9fl oz) double or regular cream (measured before whisking)

Equipment

This can be frozen in a bowl or tub or it can be made into an ice-cream 'cake' if you freeze it in a 20cm (8in) spring-form cake tin that you've lined with a double layer of cling film

Place the water and sugar in a small saucepan and heat gently until the sugar has dissolved. Remove from the heat and add the chocolate, stirring until smooth. Then stir in the peanut butter. Set aside to cool.

Place a saucepan with a few centimetres of water on a medium heat. Put the eggs and sugar into a bowl and sit it over the saucepan so that the water is not touching the bottom of the bowl. I use a heatproof glass bowl for this – a stainless-steel one is not a good idea, as it will get too hot and scramble the eggs.

Using either a hand whisk or a hand-held electric beater, whisk the eggs and sugar over the simmering water for about 5–10 minutes until the mixture is pale, light and will hold a figure of eight. Believe it or not, this is not difficult to do by hand, and will be necessary if your hand-held electric beater cannot reach your hob. Once it's holding a figure of eight, take the water off the heat and continue to whisk for about 8–10 minutes until the mixture has cooled down to room temperature.

Whip the cream in a mixing bowl until just holding stiff peaks. Too stiff and it will go grainy, too soft and it won't be able to hold the sugar mousse mixture.

Tip one quarter of the sugar mousse mixture in and fold to combine, then tip this mixture into the cream along with the vanilla extract and gently fold until it has mixed completely, but is still light and airy.

Tip into the bowl, tub or prepared tin, then pour in the peanut butter chocolate sauce and swirl through the mixture, keeping it marbled by not mixing together too thoroughly. Place in the freezer for about 6 hours or overnight, until frozen.

I love a really good oat bar, and this one ticks all the boxes for me – dense, chewy, and oh-so-packed with goodness. The tahini paste really packs a sesame punch, while the dried cranberries add their own distinctive rich sweetness.

Honey, cranberry and sesame oat bars

MAKES ABOUT 24 BARS

300g (11oz) rolled (porridge) oats

100g (3½oz) sesame seeds

50g (2oz) plain flour

200g (7oz) butter

300g (11oz) honey

150g (5oz) soft dark brown sugar

150g (5oz) dried cranberries

125g (4½oz) light tahini

Equipment

33 x 23cm (13 x 9in) Swiss roll tin

Preheat the oven to 180°C (350°F), Gas mark 4. Line the Swiss roll tin with baking parchment, leaving a little hanging over the edges for easy removal.

Place the oats, sesame seeds and flour in a large bowl and mix together.

Place the butter and honey in a saucepan on a medium heat. Stir together until melted and mixed, then stir in the sugar until it has dissolved. Add the cranberries and tahini and mix well.

Pour the butter mixture over the dry ingredients and mix very well. Tip into the prepared tin, spread out evenly, then place in the oven and bake for 20–25 minutes until golden and just set in the centre.

Remove from the oven and allow to cool in the tin, then cut into bars to serve.

FRESH & FRUITY

Blueberry jelly and milk ice cream

———————————————

Middle-Eastern orange, pistachio and
pomegranate

———————————————

Pink grapefruit and raspberries
in a light cinnamon syrup

———————————————

Yoghurt and elderflower cream
with poached rhubarb

———————————————

Watermelon with mangoes and
apricots in ginger

———————————————

Lemon verbena sorbet

———————————————

Sweet labneh with honey, pistachios and
orange blossom water

———————————————

Ivan's strawberries in red Burgundy syrup

———————————————

Prosecco and raspberry jelly

———————————————

Watermelon ginita

———————————————

Poached peaches with raspberry sherbet

———————————————

Jelly and ice cream: a classic twosome – and for very good reason, too. As the cool, refreshing ice cream starts to melt into the thick, wobbly jelly, it's hard not to feel a little nostalgic for 1980s birthday parties! This delicious combination isn't just for the children, though.

Blueberry jelly and milk ice cream

SERVES 4

For the milk ice cream

150g (5oz) caster or granulated sugar

Big pinch of salt flakes

500ml (18fl oz) milk

2 egg whites

250ml (9fl oz) double or regular cream

For the blueberry jelly

250g (9oz) blueberries

Juice of 1 lemon

75g (3oz) caster or granulated sugar

1 sheet of gelatine

Equipment

Ice-cream machine

Place the sugar, salt and milk in a saucepan over a medium heat. Stir together until the sugar has just dissolved, then set aside.

In a clean, dry bowl, whisk the egg whites until slightly fluffy (a minute or two is fine). Add the cream to the milk mixture, then combine with the egg white.

Freeze in an ice-cream machine according to the manufacturer's instructions.

Place the blueberries and lemon juice in a blender and whiz for a good few minutes until very smooth. Then push through a sieve and set aside.

Place 50ml (2fl oz) water and the sugar in a saucepan over a medium heat. Stir just until the sugar has dissolved, then remove from the heat and set aside.

Place the gelatine in a bowl of cold water and leave to sit for 3–5 minutes until softened. Remove the gelatine sheet from its soaking water and squeeze out any excess liquid. Transfer the softened gelatine to the warm syrup and stir until dissolved. Add some 4 or 5 tablespoons of the blueberry-lemon liquid to the gelatine syrup and stir together. Then pour the mixture into the remaining blueberry liquid.

Stir everything together well, then divide among four glasses or moulds and place in the fridge to set. This should take 3–4 hours.

Serve the blueberry jelly with the milk ice cream.

Fresh, fragrant and delightfully simple, this little concoction is a delicious way to start the day or, indeed, to end a meal.

Middle-Eastern orange, pistachio and pomegranate

SERVES 4

4 oranges

30g (1¼oz) icing sugar

2 tbsp orange blossom water

2–3 tbsp crème fraîche or sour cream

½–1 pomegranate, seeds removed

25g (1oz) pistachios, toasted (see tip on page 28) and chopped

Cut the top and bottom off the oranges, just down as far as the flesh. Peel the oranges with a knife, either from the top to bottom or in a spiral around the Equator. Cut the oranges into slices horizontally.

Place the oranges in a bowl, then sprinkle the icing sugar and the orange blossom water over the top. Place in the fridge for at least 1 hour (or even the whole day) to chill.

When ready to serve, put on plates, spoon a blob of crème fraîche over the oranges and sprinkle with the pomegranate seeds and the pistachios.

I remember the American mum of one of my school friends used to eat a half grapefruit sprinkled with cinnamon for breakfast every morning. This is not only a very healthy way to start the day, it's also a really good flavour match, which gave me the inspiration for this recipe. The cool, tangy flavours from the pink grapefruit and raspberries are injected with a sunny warmth from the sweet cinnamon.

Pink grapefruit and raspberries in a light cinnamon syrup

SERVES 4

75g (3oz) caster or granulated sugar

½ cinnamon stick or ⅛ tsp ground cinnamon

2 pink grapefruit

125g (4½oz) raspberries

Heat the sugar and 75ml (3fl oz) water with the cinnamon until the sugar has dissolved, then reduce the heat and simmer for a few minutes. Remove from the heat and set aside for about an hour to allow the cinnamon to infuse.

Meanwhile, peel and segment the grapefruit. Using a small, sharp knife and working over a bowl to catch the juices, cut off the ends, then carefully cut away the peel and pith in a spiral until you have a peeled grapefruit with only flesh and no pith. Next, carefully cut along the edge of each segment, leaving behind the membrane and freeing a segment of flesh from the pith. Repeat for all the segments and place the flesh in a bowl with the raspberries, squeezing over every last bit of juice from the peel and the membrane.

Remove the cinnamon stick from the syrup, if using, then pour the syrup over the fruit and chill in the fridge.

Serve chilled in little bowls or glasses as a delicious and refreshing dessert.

Nature is the perfect matchmaker. Think tomato and basil, blackberry and apple, and pea and mint. This recipe, which is a wonderfully refreshing take on an Italian panna cotta, gives a nod to the late spring/early summer elderflowers and rhubarb.

Yoghurt and elderflower cream with poached rhubarb

SERVES 6

150ml (5fl oz) milk

130ml (4½fl oz) double or regular cream

120g (4oz) caster or granulated sugar

2 sheets of gelatine

280ml (9½fl oz) yoghurt

120ml (4fl oz) elderflower cordial

For the poached rhubarb

225g (8oz) caster or granulated sugar

225ml (8fl oz) water

450g (1lb) trimmed rhubarb stalks, sliced 2cm thick

350g (12oz) hulled, sliced strawberries

Place the milk, cream and sugar in a saucepan on a medium–low heat. Warm, and stir until the sugar has just dissolved, then remove from the heat.

Soften the gelatine in a bowl of cold water for 3–5 minutes, then remove the gelatine sheet from its soaking water and squeeze out any excess liquid. Add the softened gelatine to the warm milk mixture and stir until dissolved.

Combine the yoghurt and elderflower cordial in a bowl, then gently whisk in the warm milk mixture. Transfer to a bowl or individual glasses and place in the fridge to set for about 3 hours.

Meanwhile, poach the rhubarb. Place the sugar and water in a saucepan over a medium–high heat. Stir as it comes to the boil to dissolve the sugar. Once it is boiling, tip in the rhubarb and stir gently. Bring the syrup back up to a gentle boil, cover with a lid and cook for just 1 minute, stirring gently once or twice without breaking up the rhubarb. Take off the heat, leave the lid on and set aside to cool. It will carry on cooking as it sits, but hopefully the rhubarb will hold its shape.

When the rhubarb is soft, with no bite, gently tip it and all the juices into a serving bowl. Add in the sliced strawberries, barely stirring them in. Set aside for at least half an hour before serving. The poached rhubarb is also divine served with meringues and cream.

Truly refreshing, this colourful combination is a great way to finish off a rich or heavy meal with some added ginger to kick-start the digestion.

Watermelon with mangoes and apricots in ginger

SERVES 4–6

100g (3½oz) caster or granulated sugar

50g (2oz) root ginger, peeled and sliced finely

4 apricots

1 mango

¼ watermelon

Place 200ml (7fl oz) water, the sugar and ginger in a small saucepan on a medium heat. Bring to the boil, then reduce the heat, simmer for 2 minutes and set aside to cool.

Slice the apricots towards the stone to form about eight segments per fruit. Peel the mango and slice into nice thin slices, again towards the stone. Cut the flesh of the watermelon off the skin, then slice into segments, then into chunks, removing any seeds. Place all the fruit in a bowl and pour over the syrup.

Chill in the fridge and serve as a lovely refreshing dessert.

If you don't have some lemon verbena in a pot by a sunny window or planted up against a south-facing wall, then may I please recommend you go out and get one right now? My favourite of all the summer herbs to infuse in boiling water for a refreshing tissane, lemon verbena comes into its own when made into a sorbet. And for a proper celebration, a dash of something pink and bubbly over the top will have you jumping for joy!

Lemon verbena sorbet

SERVES 8

225g (8oz) caster or granulated sugar

2 sprigs of lemon verbena

Juice of 3 lemons

1 egg white (optional)

Equipment

Ice-cream machine or sorbetière (optional)

Place the sugar, 600ml (1 pint) water and the lemon verbena sprigs in a saucepan over a medium–low heat. Bring slowly to the boil and simmer for 3 minutes. Remove from the heat and take out the lemon verbena sprigs. Allow the syrup to get quite cold, then add the strained juice of 3 lemons.

Strain and freeze in an ice-cream machine or sorbetière. If you don't have an ice-cream machine or sorbetière, simply freeze the sorbet in a freezable bowl. When it is semi-frozen, whisk until smooth and return to the freezer. Whisk again when almost frozen and fold in the stiffly beaten egg white.

If you have access to a food processor, you can simply freeze the sorbet completely in a tray, then break up and whiz for a few seconds in the processor. Drop the slightly beaten egg white down the tube, whiz and freeze again. Keep in the freezer until needed.

Serve in chilled glasses or chilled bowls. If you like, you can splash over a little pink prosecco.

Rachel's Tip: Lemon balm or mint could be used in place of the lemon verbena.

Labneh is a Middle-Eastern delicacy that is simply strained yoghurt, though sometimes it is called yoghurt cheese. Because of the fact that a lot of the whey has gone in the straining, it can be cooked without curdling. But it is like this that I love it most: as a completely simple dish to have at the end of the meal, or even for breakfast, with just some honey, nuts and, if you wish, a drizzle of fragrant orange blossom or rose water.

Sweet labneh with honey, pistachios and orange blossom water

SERVES 3–4

600g (1lb 5oz) natural yoghurt

2 tsp honey

25g (1oz) pistachios, toasted (see tip on page 28) and chopped

1 tsp orange blossom water

Place a sheet of kitchen paper in a sieve sitting over a bowl, then tip the yoghurt into it. Place in the fridge and allow to drip for 3 hours or overnight. It will thicken as it sits and the liquid drips through.

Next, discard or drink the liquid in the bowl, then tip the thick yoghurt (labneh) into the bowl. Stir in half of the honey, then put it on a large plate or individual plates and drizzle the remaining honey over the top. Scatter with the pistachios and orange blossom water and serve.

Rachel's Tips: You could use rose water instead of orange blossom water and add a few pomegranate seeds over the top.

Another gem from Isaac's cousin Ivan, this recipe came back to Ireland with him from France in the late 1980s after he spent a few months learning French in Tours. The ripe red berry and sweet black cherry notes from Burgundy's Pinot Noir wines work so well with strawberries. Pinot Noirs from other parts of the world will be successful here, too.

Ivan's strawberries in red Burgundy syrup

SERVES 4

75g (3oz) caster or granulated sugar

150ml (5fl oz) light, fruity red Burgundy, other Pinot Noir or maybe a Beaujolais

300g (11oz) strawberries, sliced

Place the sugar and 100ml (3½fl oz) water in a saucepan on a medium heat. Stir together until just dissolved, then allow to cool for a few minutes. Next, stir in the Burgundy and chill in the fridge for at least 2 hours. Add the sliced strawberries and leave for a further 2 hours in the fridge before serving.

Rachel's Tip: To set as a jelly, soften 1½ sheets of gelatine in cold water for 3–5 minutes, then dissolve the squeezed-out sheets of gelatine in 100ml (3½fl oz) of the warm Burgundy syrup. Keep this syrup out of the fridge while the rest of the syrup chills. When the syrup in the fridge is cold, pour 100ml (3½fl oz) of the cold syrup into the gelatine syrup mix and mix it all back in with the cold syrup. Add the strawberries into the syrup and transfer into pretty glasses to set.

Prosecco and jelly: two of my favourite things. And when combined with raspberries, they make a wickedly celebratory concoction. The reason for putting this in the freezer for the first half an hour is to help set the prosecco bubbles in the jelly. It also works very well with cava.

Prosecco and raspberry jelly

SERVES 4

3 sheets of gelatine

50g (2oz) caster or granulated sugar

375ml bottle of prosecco

125g (4½oz) raspberries

Place your chosen glasses or bowls in the freezer for half an hour. Soften the gelatine sheets in a bowl of cold water for 3–5 minutes.

Place 2 tablespoons of water and the sugar in a saucepan over a medium–low heat. Stir until the sugar dissolves, then remove from the heat.

Remove the gelatine sheets from their soaking water and squeeze out any excess liquid. Transfer the softened gelatine to the hot syrup and stir until dissolved. Set aside to cool for 5 minutes, then pour the prosecco into the syrup. Remove the glasses or bowls from the freezer, pour in the jelly mixture and return to the freezer for half an hour.

Take the glasses out of the freezer and place 8–10 raspberries in each jelly, pressing down slightly. Chill the jellies in the fridge for 2–3 hours until fully set.

Rachel's Tip: The two freezing stages help keep the prosecco bubbles in the jelly. If you prefer, you can use normal white wine and skip these steps.

A granita with gin – what could be more divine?! If you love a slice of cucumber in your gin and tonic, then be sure to include it here. Delicious before or after a meal or simply as a little refreshment on a balmy evening.

Watermelon ginita

SERVES 4-6

500g (1lb 2oz) watermelon flesh (about ¼ watermelon)

30g (1oz) peeled and seeded cucumber (optional)

Juice of 1 lime

100ml (3½fl oz) gin

1–2 tsp sugar, to taste (optional)

Pick out the seeds from the watermelon and discard. Place the flesh in a food processor with the cucumber, if using. Blitz with the lime juice and gin until smooth, then push through a sieve. Taste, and if necessary, add a teaspoon or two of sugar.

Transfer to a freezable container and freeze. Whisk the mixture several times during the freezing process.

Rachel's Tips: Ring the changes on a summer's day and add peaches, nectarines or apricots to the ginita. You can also leave out the gin for a non-alcoholic granita.

Possibly my favourite recipe in the book, this takes its inspiration from the classic Peach Melba, which was created by the King of Chefs, Frenchman Auguste Escoffier, for the Australian opera singer Dame Nellie Melba. Peaches and raspberries are a match made in heaven and this sherbet, which is neither a sorbet nor an ice cream but something in between, is the perfect accompaniment.

Poached peaches with raspberry sherbet

SERVES 4

For the raspberry sherbet

150g (5oz) raspberries, fresh or frozen

150ml (5fl oz) milk

60g (2½oz) caster or granulated sugar

4 tbsp lemon juice

For the poached peaches

100g (3½oz) caster or granulated sugar

4 peaches

Equipment

Ice-cream machine (optional)

To make the sherbet, place the raspberries, milk, sugar and lemon juice in a blender and whiz until smooth. Push through a fine sieve. Taste and add more sugar or lemon juice if necessary – you're tasting for a balance between sweet and sharp.

Freeze in an ice-cream machine according to the manufacturer's instructions. Alternatively, freeze in the freezer and take out three times during freezing to beat with a whisk or fork (to break up the ice crystals) before covering again and placing back in the freezer.

Place the sugar and 100ml (3½fl oz) water in a saucepan and bring to the boil, stirring to dissolve the sugar. Cut the peaches in half, remove the stones and tip the peaches into the syrup. Cover with a lid and cook on a medium heat for 10–12 minutes, until the peaches are tender but not yet falling apart. Then remove from the heat and allow to cool. The skins will have come off during cooking, so remove them completely and discard.

Serve with the raspberry sherbet.

MINI MOUTHFULS

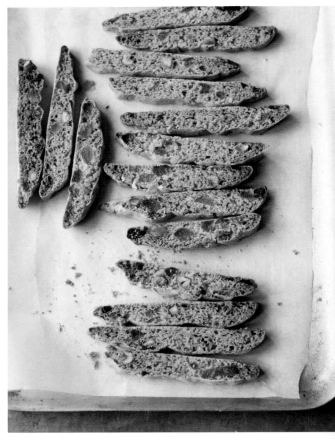

Ginger crunch

Cinnamon cigars

Chocolate and candied orange dates

JR's rose water marshmallows

Ballymaloe vanilla fudge

Chocolate fruit and nut clusters

Baklava

Pistachio, apricot and cardamom biscotti

Sesame and honey halva

A New Zealand classic, these divine little treats are the perfect accompaniment to a great cup of coffee. The crunchy, gingery shortbread base and the smooth ginger fudge topping take no time to throw together, but happily last very well for over a week. They can be cut into squares, fingers or little morsels that you'll just keep going back to, time and time again.

Ginger crunch

MAKES ABOUT 50 MINI TREATS OR 28 SLICES

For the base

225g (8oz) plain flour

100g (3½oz) caster sugar

2 tsp ground ginger

1 tsp baking powder

150g (5oz) butter, cut into cubes

For the topping

150g (5oz) butter

100g (3½oz) golden syrup

300g (11oz) icing sugar

2 tbsp ground ginger

Equipment

23 x 33cm (9 x 13in) tin

Preheat the oven to 180°C/350°F/Gas 4. Line the tin with baking parchment.

Place the flour, caster sugar, ginger and baking powder in a food processor and whiz to mix, then add in the butter and whiz again until it almost comes together. Alternatively, rub the butter into the dry ingredients by hand until the mixture resembles coarse breadcrumbs.

Tip into the prepared baking tin and press to evenly cover the base. Bake for 20 minutes until light golden.

About 5 minutes before the pastry is ready, place the butter and golden syrup in a saucepan on a medium–high heat and melt together. Add in the icing sugar and the ground ginger and cook for just 1–2 minutes until combined.

Pour the warm topping over the cooked base just after it comes out of the oven and allow to cool. Cut into slices or small squares to serve.

Puff pastry, icing sugar and cinnamon – just three simple ingredients. But believe me, these are much more than a sum of their parts. All you need is a pot of coffee and a few friends.

Cinnamon cigars

MAKES 12 CIGARS

1 tsp ground cinnamon

25g (1oz) icing sugar

200g (7oz) puff pastry

Preheat the oven to 220°C (425°F), Gas mark 7. Line a baking tray with baking parchment.

In a small bowl, mix together the cinnamon and icing sugar.

Roll out the puff pastry into a neat rectangle about 20 x 30cm (8 x 12in). Cut it into 12 rectangles, each about 5 x 10cm (2 x 4in). Sprinkle each small rectangle with about ½ teaspoon of the cinnamon sugar, then roll into a little cigar shape. Dust the outside with a little more cinnamon sugar, then place on the baking tray. Place in the fridge to chill for 15 minutes.

Place the tray in the oven and bake for 8–12 minutes until puffed and golden brown.

Rachel's Tip: Perfect for using up scraps of puff pastry.

I absolutely adored visiting the date market in Abu Dhabi, and literally ate my way around. I was intrigued by the huge variety of dates, from small and intense-tasting to plump and toffee-flavoured. There were dates stuffed with everything from caramelised nuts to candied fruit and some were dipped in chocolate, too. I made these when I returned home to give me a little taste of the exotic Middle East.

Chocolate and candied orange dates

MAKES 12 DATES

125g (4½oz) dark chocolate (55–70% cocoa solids), chopped or in pieces/drops

12 dates (Medjool dates are fabulous for this)

12 pieces of candied orange peel, about 1 x 2cm (½ x ¾in) in size, so they fit snugly in the dates

Place the chocolate in a bowl sitting over a saucepan with a few centimetres of water. Bring the water up to the boil, then take off the heat and allow the chocolate to melt slowly.

Meanwhile, place a piece of baking parchment on a baking tray.

Split the dates in half, but not all the way through. Remove the stones and discard, then stuff the dates with a piece (or a few small pieces if that's the size of your peel) of candied peel. Close the dates again, pinching the edges to seal.

Using two forks, dip each date in the melted chocolate, then transfer each one (so they're not touching each other) to the paper-lined tray. Place somewhere cool for the chocolate to set.

JR Ryall is the fabulously talented and super-lovely pastry chef at Ballymaloe House. He creates the most delicious sweet things for the dessert trolley, all with the same sensitivity and elegant touch as that of my husband's grandmother, Myrtle Allen, who opened the restaurant in 1964 and who still presides over the place today. Petits fours are served at the end of every evening meal at Ballymaloe and this recipe is just one of JR's gems.

JR's rose water marshmallows

MAKES ABOUT 90
MARSHMALLOWS

75g (3oz) icing sugar

75g (3oz) cornflour

455g (1lb) caster or granulated sugar

1 tbsp liquid or powdered glucose

9 sheets of gelatine or 9 tsp powdered gelatine

2 egg whites

2 tbsp rose water

Few drops of red food colouring (optional)

Equipment

30 x 20cm (12 x 8in) baking tray and a sugar thermometer

Line the baking tray with baking parchment. Sift the icing sugar and cornflour together.

Place the sugar, glucose and 200ml (7fl oz) water in a heavy-based saucepan. Stir to ensure all of the sugar is wet. Using a pastry brush dipped in water, remove any sugar crystals from the side of the saucepan. Place the saucepan on a medium heat and bring to the boil. Once boiling, do not stir, simply tilt the pan from side to side to ensure that the solution heats evenly until it reaches 127°C (261°F).

Meanwhile, soak the gelatine in 140ml (5fl oz) cold water for 3–5 minutes.

When the boiling syrup reaches 110°C (230°F), start whipping the egg whites in the bowl of an electric food mixer until stiff peaks form.

Add the gelatine and its soaking liquid into the syrup when it reaches 127°C (261°F) and stir with a wooden spoon. The mixture will foam slightly – this is normal. Whisking constantly, pour the hot syrup onto the egg whites and whip on full speed for 5–10 minutes until the marshmallow thickens and the bowl of the mixer has cooled to a tepid heat. Add the rose water and food colouring, if using, and continue to mix just until mixed through.

Cont. overleaf

Spoon the marshmallow mix into the lined baking tray and smooth with a palette knife. Allow to set for about 1–2 hours.

Dust the marshmallows with one-third of the icing sugar and cornflour mix. Turn out onto a work surface, cut into 2cm (¾in) squares and toss in the remaining icing sugar and flour.

These marshmallows will keep for up to 1 week.

Variation: **Raspberry marshmallows**
Omit the rose water and red food colouring and add 1 tsp vanilla extract instead. When you tip the mixture onto the tray, only pour out half, then scatter 250g (9oz) fresh raspberries evenly over the mixture, pour over the other half and allow to set. These are best eaten within 24 hours.

Another variation (too good not to include!): **Coconut marshmallows**
Omit the rose water and red food colouring and add 70ml (3fl oz) Malibu instead. Toast 150g (5oz) desiccated coconut by spreading out on a baking tray and cooking at 170°C (325°F), Gas mark 3 for 4–7 minutes until light golden. Toss the cut marshmallows in the toasted coconut instead of the icing sugar and cornflour.

This is the original fudge recipe that has been made at Ballymaloe House for more than a few decades now. When something is so good, why change it? Crumbly, wickedly sweet and with just the perfect amount of vanilla, this recipe is a knock-out.

Ballymaloe vanilla fudge

MAKES ABOUT
96 SQUARES

225g (8oz) butter

1 x 410g (14½oz) tin of evaporated milk

900g (2lb) caster sugar

3 tsp vanilla extract

Equipment

23 x 33cm (9 x 13in) Swiss roll tin and a sugar thermometer (optional)

Melt the butter in a heavy-based saucepan over a low heat. Add the evaporated milk, 200ml (7fl oz) water, sugar and vanilla extract and stir with a whisk until the sugar is dissolved. Turn up the heat to simmer and stir often for about 35–45 minutes. It's ready when it reaches 115°C (239°F). If you have a sugar thermometer, use it as soon as the mixture boils. If you don't have one, test for the soft ball stage (to do this, place a blob – ½ teaspoon or so – in a small bowl of cold water; as it cools, it will form a soft ball).

Pull off the heat and stir until it thickens and reaches the required consistency, with the saucepan set in a bowl of cold water. Allow to set for 2 minutes and then stir to break up any sugar crystals. Pour into the Swiss roll tin and smooth out with a spatula.

Allow to cool a little, then cut before completely cold.

The simplest of all mini treats to make, these are just a slightly more grown-up version of the birthday party staple: chocolate Rice Krispies cakes. Feel free to play to your heart's content with different filling combinations. Absolutely divine with a cup of coffee or a glass of liqueur at the end of a meal, or just a quick treat on the run.

Chocolate fruit and nut clusters

MAKES 25 SMALL CLUSTERS

125g (4½oz) dark chocolate (55–70% cocoa solids),

50g (2oz) toasted nuts, chopped (see tip on page 28)

50g (2oz) dried fruits, chopped

Place a sheet of baking parchment on a baking tray.

To melt the chocolate, place the chocolate in a bowl sitting over a saucepan with a few centimetres of water. Bring the water up to the boil, then take off the heat and allow the chocolate to melt slowly.

Stir in your chosen nuts and dried fruit, then use two teaspoons to make small clusters on the paper. Place somewhere cool to set.

Combinations that work well are

Pecan and cranberry
Hazelnut and fig
Pistachio and apricot
Almond and date
White chocolate, candied orange peel and stem ginger

Ever since I backpacked around a few of the Greek islands when I was twenty, I have adored baklava. Sweet, a little bit spicy and oh-so-nutty, this is well worth making for the baklava-lover in your life. Even if that person is you.

Baklava

MAKES ABOUT
28 BAKLAVA

110g (4oz) caster sugar

200g (7oz) ground almonds

3 tsp ground cinnamon

150g (5oz) butter, melted

200g (7oz) filo pastry

For the syrup

340g (12oz) caster or granulated sugar

200g (7oz) honey

½ cinnamon stick

8 cloves

Equipment

20cm (8in) square tin

Preheat the oven to 180°C (350°F), Gas mark 4.

In a bowl, mix together the sugar, almonds and cinnamon.

Line the base and sides of the tin with baking parchment. Brush the lined tin with some of the melted butter. Cut the filo the same size as the tin, then place four layers of filo in the base of the tin, brushing more melted butter over each layer.

Sprinkle half of the almond mix on top of the last buttered sheet, place one more sheet on top and butter it, and then sprinkle over the remaining half of the almond mix. If you have any offcuts of filo pastry, use these in the first four layers of pastry.

Set another four to six layers of filo on top, buttering between each layer. Cut the baklava diagonally into 3–4cm (1¼–1½in) diamonds in the tray.

Sprinkle with a teaspoon of water, then place in the oven and bake for 1½ hours until golden.

While the baklava bakes, make the syrup. Mix all of the ingredients together with 175ml (6fl oz) water in a saucepan and place over a medium–high heat. Bring to the boil and boil for 10 minutes.

When the baklava is baked, pour over the boiling syrup.

Cut down through the baklava where you have cut before baking. Set aside and allow to cool for a few hours or overnight.

Rachel's Tip: If the square tin has a removable base, the baklava in the tin should be placed on a baking tray in case it seeps a little as it cools.

Biscotti are such good-humoured little biscuits. This recipe makes loads, you can play around with the different fruit, nuts and spices, and they last for weeks in an airtight box or jar. I particularly love the dried apricot, pistachio and cardamom combo here and, of course, they can also be dipped in melted chocolate.

Pistachio, apricot and cardamom biscotti

MAKES ABOUT 40 BISCOTTI

100g (3½oz) plain flour, plus extra for dusting

100g (3½oz) caster sugar

1 tsp baking powder

½ tsp ground cardamom seeds

1 egg, beaten

50g (2oz) shelled, roasted and salted pistachios

50g (2oz) dried apricots, sliced into 6 pieces

Preheat the oven to 170°C (325°F), Gas mark 3.

Sift together the flour, sugar and baking powder into a large bowl. Stir in the ground cardamom, then mix in the beaten egg to form a soft dough. Next, mix in the pistachios and apricots.

Flour your hands, then turn the dough onto a lightly floured work surface and form into a sausage about 30cm (12in) long and 3cm (1¼in) wide. Place on a baking tray and bake for about 25 minutes, then remove and allow to cool on a wire rack for 5 minutes.

Cut into slices about 5mm (¼in) thick, then lay flat on the tray and bake for a further 10 minutes. Turn all the biscotti over on the tray, then return to the oven and continue to bake for 10 minutes more. They should be a light golden colour on both cut sides.

Cool on a wire rack, then transfer to an airtight container where they will keep for up to three weeks.

Halva, which in Arabic means 'sweet' or 'desserts', is made in many parts of the world, including the Middle East, Asia, North Africa and Eastern Europe. There are a few different types, but perhaps the most well-known one is that made from the über-nutritious sesame seed paste, tahini. The last time I was in Istanbul I ate nearly my body weight of the stuff! Happily, it's very easy and quick to make, too.

Sesame and honey halva

SERVES 8-10

300g (11oz) honey

250g (9oz) light tahini paste (stirred well to mix in any excess oil)

Equipment

900g (2lb) loaf tin

Sugar thermometer (optional)

Line the base and sides of a loaf tin with baking parchment.

Place the honey in a small to medium saucepan on a high heat and bring up to the boil. Continue to boil for 8–10 minutes, stirring regularly. It's ready when it reaches 115°C (239°F). If you have a sugar thermometer, use it as soon as the honey boils. If you don't have one, test for the soft ball stage (to do this, place a blob – ½ teaspoon or so – in a small bowl of cold water; as it cools, it will form a soft ball).

Cool for 3 minutes off the heat, then stir in the tahini paste and pour into the lined tin.

When completely cool, cover and place in the fridge. Leave to sit for 36 hours to allow the small sugar crystals that give halva its distinctive texture time to develop.

Cut into chunks or slabs to serve.

SOMETHING FOR THE AFTERNOON

Cinnamon spiral buns

Vanilla custard slice

Lavender sponge cake with rhubarb curd

Double chocolate pecan blondies

Sinead's Louise slice

Banana, ginger and golden syrup bread

Mango and lime drizzle cake

Salted caramel cupcakes

Lemon slab cake

Orange and almond cake

Lemon yoghurt polenta cake

Pear and nutmeg cake

Afternoon fruit brack

If ever I open a cute little tea shop, these will always be on the menu. A large 'cake' of individual buns, each their own spiral around sweet, sticky cinnamon butter, all topped with a drizzle of icing.

Cinnamon spiral buns

SERVES 10

80g (3oz) butter, plus extra for greasing

15g (½oz) fresh yeast or 1 x 7g (¼oz) sachet of fast-action yeast or 2 tsp of dried yeast

150–200ml (5–7fl oz) tepid water

450g (1lb) strong white flour, plus extra for dusting

Pinch of salt

35g (1¼oz) caster sugar

1 egg, beaten

For the cinnamon butter

125g (4½oz) butter

125g (4½oz) icing sugar

1 tsp ground cinnamon

For the icing

100g (3½oz) icing sugar

Equipment

23cm (9in) spring-form cake tin

Line the base of the cake tin with baking parchment and butter the sides. Dissolve the yeast in 50ml (2fl oz) of the water. Allow to sit for a few minutes.

In a separate bowl, sift together the flour and salt and add in the sugar. Rub in the butter with your fingers, then add in the egg. Add the yeast and combine with enough water to form a fairly soft dough. Knead well for 5–10 minutes until the dough becomes smooth and springs back when pressed – this will only take 5 minutes if using a food mixer with a dough hook. Place in a bowl and cover with cling film, then allow to rise until doubled in size (about 1½ hours). Knock back by kneading for 1–2 minutes, then rest briefly before rolling into a 30 x 40cm (12 x 16in) rectangle on a floured work surface.

Next, make the cinnamon butter. Beat the butter until very soft, then add in the icing sugar and cinnamon. Spread this cinnamon butter over the surface of the dough rectangle. Starting at the long end, and using two hands, roll the dough away from you. When it's rolled, cut ten slices, each about 3cm (1¼in) wide (the dough will have shrunk back a little). Place cut side up in the tin, with nine around the edge and one in the centre. Cover with a tea towel and place somewhere warm to rise for about 1 hour (or in the fridge overnight) or until the buns are doubled in size and when you press gently with your finger, your mark stays indented.

Preheat the oven to 180°C (350°F), Gas mark 4. When the buns have risen, take off the tea towel and place in the oven for 30–40 minutes until cooked in the centre. Allow to sit for 5 minutes before taking out of the tin and placing on a wire rack.

Make the icing by mixing together the icing sugar with 1–1½ tablespoons water, adding just enough water to form a drizzling consistency. Finish the buns by drizzling over the icing in a criss-cross pattern, then allow to set.

Probably the most 'retro' recipe in the book – two layers of buttery puff pastry sandwiching sweet vanilla custard and topped with a white glacé icing. Bring back the custard slice, I say!

Vanilla custard slice

MAKES 8 SLICES

300g (11oz) puff pastry

For the crème pâtissière (pastry cream)

375ml (13fl oz) milk

1 vanilla pod, split down the middle, or 1 tsp vanilla extract

75g (3oz) caster sugar

3 egg yolks

40g (1½oz) cornflour

Pinch of salt

25g (1oz) butter, cut into small cubes

For the icing

150g (5oz) icing sugar

50g (2oz) dark chocolate (55–70% cocoa solids), roughly chopped

First, make the crème pâtissière. Pour the milk into a saucepan and add the split vanilla pod, if using. If using the vanilla extract, add it in with the butter at the end. Bring the milk mixture to the boil, then remove from the heat.

Whisk the sugar, egg yolks and cornflour together in a large bowl for about 2–3 minutes using a hand-held electric beater or electric food mixer until pale and light.

Next, pour the hot milk onto the egg mixture, whisking continuously, then return the mixture to the saucepan. Cook the mixture over a low heat, stirring continuously, until the mixture boils and becomes thick. It will just come to the boil. If it boils unevenly or too quickly, it may become lumpy, in which case use a whisk to mix until smooth again.

Remove the custard from the heat and pour into a bowl (push the mixture through a sieve if there are any lumps). Add the pinch of salt and the butter and stir until melted and thoroughly combined.

Leave to cool, cover with cling film and then chill before using.

Preheat the oven to 220°C (425°F), Gas mark 7. Line two baking trays with baking parchment.

Divide the pastry into two equal pieces and roll out both pieces to 20cm (8in) square and 3mm (⅛in) thick. If you're using a sheet of ready-rolled pastry, the chances are it may be a rectangle measuring 18 x 46cm (7 x 18in). In which case, cut it in half so that you have two 23 x 18cm (9 x 7in) pieces, then roll each piece to about 20cm (8in) square. Place each pastry sheet on a lined baking tray, prick each piece a few times with a fork and chill for 10–15 minutes.

Bake the pastry sheets for 10–15 minutes or until golden brown and crisp. Set aside to cool.

Place one pastry sheet on a lined baking tray (reserve the prettiest piece for the top).

Spread the crème pâtissière evenly over the pastry on the baking tray, then place the other piece of pastry on top. Refrigerate while making the icing.

For the icing, sift the icing sugar into a bowl. Stir in 3–4 teaspoons cold water – just enough to give you a thick, drizzling consistency – and set aside.

Place the chocolate in a bowl sitting over a saucepan with a few centimetres of water. Bring the water up to the boil, then take off the heat and allow the chocolate to melt slowly. Once cooled slightly, transfer the melted chocolate into a piping bag fitted with a very small, plain nozzle.

Take the custard slice from the fridge and spread the icing over the top layer of pastry. A palette knife or spatula dipped into boiling water is handy for helping the icing to spread.

Using the piping bag, draw ten parallel lines with the melted chocolate along the top of the icing in one direction. Using the top of a toothpick, 'drag' the lines of chocolate across the icing in alternating directions at about 2cm (¾in) intervals to create a feathered effect. Place the slice back in the fridge to set. It will be easier to cut if it's been in the fridge for at least 2 hours.

Cut the finished custard slice into eight pieces, trimming the edges if you wish. Using the foil, carefully lift the portioned vanilla slices out of the tray and serve.

Rachel's Tip: If you prefer, you can just drizzle the icing and leave out the chocolate.

A gorgeously light and perfumed sponge with a seriously rhubarby curd, this has all the flavours of early summer.

Lavender sponge cake with rhubarb curd

SERVES 8

For the lavender sponge

6 eggs

175g (6oz) caster or granulated sugar

Pinch of salt

150g (5oz) plain flour

2 tsp lavender buds, finely chopped (off the stems)

125g (4½oz) butter, melted, plus extra for greasing

For the rhubarb curd

550g (1lb 3oz) rhubarb, cut in to 1cm (½in) slices (weigh when sliced and trimmed)

200g (7oz) caster or granulated sugar

75g (3oz) butter

3 eggs, whisked

Icing sugar and chopped lavender buds, to decorate

Preheat the oven to 180°C (350°F), Gas mark 4. Line the base of three 18cm (7in) cake tins and butter the sides.

To make the sponge, place the eggs, sugar and salt in a bowl and, using an electric whisk, beat for 5–8 minutes until tripled in volume, light and fluffy. Sift in the flour and fold into the light mousse-like mixture with the lavender and the melted butter, working quickly so that not too much air escapes.

Divide the cake mixture among the three tins and place in the oven. Bake for 22–25 minutes until light golden and a skewer inserted into the centre comes out clean. Take out of the oven and let sit in the tin for a few minutes before taking out and cooling on a wire rack.

Next, make the curd. Place the rhubarb and 50g (2oz) of the sugar in a saucepan on a medium heat, stirring every so often. Cook for 6–8 minutes until the rhubarb has softened, broken up completely and the mixture has thickened to a pulp.

Pour into a sieve sitting over a bowl and push the mixture through the sieve into the bowl, making sure to scrape the underside of the sieve to get every last bit.

Next, place the butter in the cleaned saucepan on a low–medium heat and allow to melt. Take off the heat and add in the eggs, the rest of the sugar and the rhubarb purée. Put back on a low heat and stir continuously for 5–7 minutes until thickened. Take off the heat, tip into a bowl and allow to cool.

Cont. opposite

Equipment

3 x 18cm (7in) cake tins
with 3cm (1¼in) sides

When ready to assemble, place one cake (save the cake with the best-looking top for the top) upside down on a plate or cake stand. Place half of the curd on top and spread it out (I like to allow the curd to drip slightly over the edges). Put the next cake, right side up, on top, then cover with the second half of the curd, as before. Finally, top with the third (and best-looking) cake. Dust with icing sugar and decorate with some more chopped lavender, if you wish.

Rachel's Tip: If you wish, you can also put whipped cream between the layers with the rhubarb curd, though only if the cake is all going to be eaten on the day it's made. Otherwise, serve it with some softly whipped cream on the side. Use the pinkest rhubarb you can find to get this beautiful colour.

Nearly as famous as both Debbie Harry and Marilyn Monroe put together, blondies, or blond brownies as they're sometimes known, have a base of brown sugar rather than melted chocolate through them. Soft, fudgy and oh-so-sweet, these will definitely make you sing.

Double chocolate pecan blondies

MAKES 16 BLONDIES

115g (4oz) butter

200g (7oz) soft light brown sugar

1 large egg

1 tsp vanilla extract

125g (4½oz) plain flour

Pinch of salt

75g (3oz) dark chocolate drops (or chopped chocolate)

50g (2oz) white chocolate drops (or chopped chocolate)

75g (3oz) pecans, chopped

Equipment

20cm (8in) square cake tin

Preheat the oven to 180°C (350°F), Gas mark 4. Line the base and sides of the cake tin with baking parchment.

Melt the butter, pour into a mixing bowl, then add the sugar and the egg and whisk to mix together. Next, add in the remaining ingredients and stir to mix. Tip into the prepared tin and bake for 25–28 minutes until dry on top, but still ever so slightly unset in the centre under the crust.

Allow to cool for at least 20 minutes before cutting into squares.

My friend Sinead Doran used to live in New Zealand. Since she's come back, she has been making these delicious biscuits with a shortbread base, jam filling and meringue topping. Every time I mentioned I loved them, she always said they were 'Louise slice'. I kept meaning to ask her for the actual recipe, as I didn't know who Louise was anyway. It turns out that Louise slice, or Louise cake as it's sometimes called, is a New Zealand national treasure. The recipe varies hugely, but this is Sinead's version and I love it.

Sinead's Louise slice

MAKES ABOUT 32 SLICES

75g (3oz) soft butter

35g (1¼oz) caster sugar

2 eggs, separated

150g (5oz) plain flour

1 tsp baking powder

175g (6oz) raspberry jam

For the topping

115g (4oz) caster sugar

35g (1¼oz) desiccated coconut

Equipment

23 x 30cm (9 x 12in) Swiss roll tin

Preheat the oven to 180°C (350°F), Gas mark 4. Line the Swiss roll tin with baking parchment.

Place the butter in a bowl and beat until soft, then add in the caster sugar, then the egg yolks (keep the whites for the topping).

Sift in the flour and baking powder and bring together to form quite a dry, crumbly dough. Spread out in the lined tray and press down to even it out. Spread the raspberry jam over the top.

Using a hand-held electric beater, whisk the sugar for the topping and the egg whites until they hold stiff peaks, then fold in the coconut and spread over the jam, being careful not to disturb the jam.

Bake in the oven for 25–30 minutes until light golden and crisp on top.

I think my love for this comfortingly sweet and delicious tea-time loaf has superseded that of banana bread. If you're a banana-bread lover, then this one is for you.

Banana, ginger and golden syrup bread

SERVES 8

110g (3½oz) butter

50g (2oz) soft brown sugar

125g (4½oz) golden syrup

2 eggs

125g (4½oz) plain flour

2 tsp baking powder

2 tbsp ground ginger

2 medium bananas, mashed

Equipment

900g (2lb) loaf tin

Preheat the oven to 180°C (350°F), Gas mark 4. Line the base and sides of the loaf tin with baking parchment.

In a bowl, cream the butter until soft, then beat in the brown sugar and golden syrup. Beat in the eggs one at a time. The mixture will look sloppy and curdled, but don't worry. Sift in the flour, baking powder and ginger and fold together.

Next, mix in the mashed bananas to form a soft, wet dough. Pour into the loaf tin, place in the oven and bake for about 45 minutes until risen, golden brown and a skewer inserted into the centre comes out clean.

When you think of how much just a small squeeze of lime transforms a juicy chunk of exotic mango, it's not surprising that this cake works so well. A delicious drizzle cake with a totally tropical taste.

Mango and lime drizzle cake

SERVES 6–8

100g (3½oz) butter, plus extra for greasing

200g (7oz) caster sugar

Finely grated zest and juice of 1 lime

2 eggs

125g (4½oz) plain flour

1 tsp baking powder

250g (9oz) mango flesh, finely chopped (from 1 medium-sized mango)

75g (3oz) granulated sugar

Equipment

20cm (8in) spring-form cake tin

Preheat the oven to 170°C (325°F), Gas mark 3. Rub the base and the sides of the spring-form cake tin with soft butter. Do not line with a disc of baking parchment and make sure the base is upside down so there is no lip and the cake can slide off easily when cooked.

In a bowl, cream together the butter and caster sugar with the lime zest. Add the eggs one by one, stirring well after each is added. Then sift in the flour and baking powder and mix to combine. Stir in the mango flesh and transfer to the prepared tin. Place in the oven and bake for 50–60 minutes until a skewer inserted into the centre comes out clean.

Meanwhile, mix together the granulated sugar and the juice of the lime in a little bowl.

When the cake is cooked, take it out of the oven, use a skewer to make holes all over the top of the cake, then spoon over the sugary lime juices. As the cake cools, this will form a zingy, crunchy top.

When the cake has cooled down to room temperature, run a small sharp knife around the outside of the cake, then unclip and remove the sides of the tin. Use a palette knife to slide the cake off the base of the tin and onto your chosen plate or cake stand.

As you bite into these cupcakes, you get three different textures all at once: salted caramel frosting sitting over a buttery, crumbly bun oozing with a sweet-and-salty toffee sauce. What's not to love?

Salted caramel cupcakes

MAKES 12 CUPCAKES

For the salted
caramel sauce

225g (8oz) caster or
granulated sugar

75g (3oz) butter

100ml (3½fl oz) double
or regular cream

1 tsp salt

For the cupcakes

150g (5oz) plain flour

25g (1oz) cornflour

1 tsp baking powder

150g (5oz) caster sugar

Pinch of salt

100g (3½oz) butter, cut
into cubes

100ml (3½fl oz) milk

1 tsp vanilla extract

2 eggs

Cont. opposite

Preheat the oven to 170°C (325°F), Gas mark 3.

First, make the salted caramel sauce. Place the sugar in a saucepan on a medium heat. Allow to heat up. As it gets quite hot you'll notice the sugar melting and starting to caramelise around the sides of the saucepan. Swirl or gently shake the pan every so often until all the sugar turns a deep golden brown and is smooth and glossy. You might need to stir it a little bit with a wooden spoon to bash out any sugary lumps. Stir in the butter and the cream and keep stirring until it is smooth again – it might take a minute or so. Add in the salt and remove from the heat.

Next, make the cupcakes. Place 12 paper cases in a cupcake/muffin tray. Sift the flour, cornflour and baking powder into a bowl, then mix in the sugar and salt. Rub in the butter. Place the milk, vanilla extract and eggs in a separate bowl and whisk to mix. Pour into the dry ingredients and bring together with a wooden spoon. Fill each paper case about two-thirds or three-quarters full, then bake in the oven for about 20–25 minutes until cooked in the centre. There should be a light spring when you gently press the centres with your finger. Take out of the oven and allow the cupcakes to cool.

While the cupcakes are cooling, make the salted caramel buttercream icing. Place all the ingredients in a mixing bowl with 175g (6oz) of the salted caramel sauce (reserving any remaining sauce for later) and beat for 10–20 seconds to mix together until light and fluffy. Set aside.

When the cupcakes have cooled, using a small, sharp knife, cut a piece out of the centre of each cupcake, measuring about 1–2cm (½–¾in) in size. Discard (or eat!) the cut-out bits of cake, then fill the 'holes' with some of the reserved salted caramel sauce.

For the salted caramel buttercream icing

475g (1lb 1oz) icing sugar

200g (7oz) butter, at room temperature

¼ tsp salt

½ tsp vanilla extract

Equipment

12-hole cupcake/muffin tray and a piping bag with a plain or fluted nozzle (or even a plastic bag with the corner cut out)

Place the salted caramel buttercream icing in the piping bag and pipe in a swirl over each cupcake. Drizzle any remaining salted caramel sauce over each iced cupcake to decorate.

Rachel's Tip: If the cooled, salted caramel sauce is too thick to drizzle over the cupcakes, you can thin it out by stirring in a tiny trickle of water.

This is the perfect picnic treat – delicious lemon sponge topped with an intensely citrussy icing. All you need is a blanket and flask of tea.

Lemon slab cake

MAKES ABOUT
24 'SLABS'

225g (8oz) butter

300g (11oz) caster or granulated sugar

2 eggs

250g (9oz) crème fraîche

Juice and finely grated zest of 1 lemon

225g (8oz) plain flour

2 tsp baking powder

For the icing

225g (8oz) icing sugar

Juice of ½ lemon

Equipment

23 x 30cm (9 x 12in) Swiss roll tin

Preheat the oven to 180°C (350°F), Gas mark 4. Line the base and sides of the tin with baking parchment.

Melt the butter on a low heat, then pour into a mixing bowl. Add in the sugar and whisk to combine, then mix in the eggs, crème fraîche, lemon juice and zest.

Sift in the flour and baking powder and fold in to mix, then tip into the prepared tin. Place in the oven and bake for 25–30 minutes or until a skewer inserted into the centre comes out clean. Allow to cool completely before icing.

To make the icing, sift the icing sugar into a bowl and add the lemon juice gradually – you may not need it all. If it's still too stiff when you've added it all, then add a tiny bit of water to bring it to a spreadable consistency.

Spread the icing over the top of the cooled cake, allow to set (about 20 minutes), then cut into slices to serve.

This is one of my favourite cakes. The ground almonds bring a wonderful moistness to the sponge, which is made even more delicious with the rich orange curd lying seductively over the top.

Orange and almond cake

SERVES 6–8

For the cake

225g (8oz) butter, plus extra for greasing

225g (8oz) caster sugar

3 large eggs

Juice and finely grated zest of 1 orange

115g (4oz) plain flour

1 tsp baking powder

115g (4oz) ground almonds

For the curd

50g (2oz) butter

Juice and finely grated zest of 2 oranges

110g (4oz) caster or granulated sugar

2 eggs

2 egg yolks

Equipment

23cm (9in) spring-form cake tin

Preheat the oven to 180°C (350°F), Gas mark 4. Line the base of the tin with baking parchment and grease the sides.

Place the butter and sugar in a bowl, then use a wooden spoon or the paddle attachment of an electric food mixer to cream together until light and fluffy. Beat in the eggs one by one, along with the orange juice and zest. Sift in the flour and baking powder, then gently fold in with the ground almonds.

Tip into the tin, then bake for 20–25 minutes until the centre feels springy to the touch. Place on a wire rack to cool, then remove from the tin.

To make the curd, place the butter in a medium pan on a medium–low heat. When melted, whisk in the orange juice and zest, sugar, eggs and egg yolks. Cook, stirring constantly, until thick enough to coat the back of a spoon. Pour into a jug and serve with the cake.

I'm always intrigued by the texture that different ingredients bring to a cake. In this Italian-inspired recipe, the natural yoghurt gives a lovely soft crumb and an ever-so-slightly tangy flavour, while the fine polenta lends a distinctly gritty bite. If you plan on keeping this cake for more than one day, then I would recommend replacing the mascarpone icing with the lemon glacé icing from the Lemon slab cake recipe (see page 147).

Lemon yoghurt polenta cake

SERVES 8

75ml (3fl oz) sunflower oil, plus extra for greasing

2 eggs

125g (4½oz) natural yoghurt

Juice and finely grated zest of 2 lemons

175g (6oz) plain flour

300g (11oz) caster sugar

175g (6oz) fine polenta (cornmeal)

2 tsp baking powder

Pinch of salt

For the lemon mascarpone icing

250g (9oz) tub of mascarpone

Juice of 1 lemon

75g (3oz) icing sugar

Equipment

23cm (9in) spring-form cake tin

Preheat the oven to 180°C (350°F), Gas mark 4. Line the base of the cake tin with baking parchment and brush a little sunflower oil around the inside.

First, make the cake. Crack the eggs into a bowl with the natural yoghurt, oil, lemon juice and zest. Whisk together to mix well, then stir in the flour, caster sugar, fine polenta, baking powder and salt.

Tip into the prepared tin and bake for 35–40 minutes until a skewer inserted into the centre comes out clean. When cooked, remove from the oven and allow to sit in the tin for 20 minutes before taking out of the tin to finish cooling.

To make the icing, whisk all ingredients together in a bowl and set aside until the cake is cool.

When ready to ice the cake, use a long-bladed (and serrated if possible) knife to split the cake in half and place the bottom half on a plate or cake stand. I find the base of the cake tin handy for sliding under and transporting each half. Spread enough of the icing to cover the bottom half (like generously buttering a piece of bread), then cover with the top half. Ice the top of the cake.

This cake can be stored (if you're keeping it any longer than a day) covered in the fridge to keep the mascarpone fresh, but make sure you bring it up to room temperature before eating it.

This recipe is inspired by a version of an old classic Dutch apple cake that's been made at Ballymaloe for nearly half a century. It's brilliant as a dessert or a perfect accompaniment to a tea or coffee.

Pear and nutmeg cake

Serves 8

2 eggs

175g (6oz) caster sugar

½ tsp vanilla extract

75g (3oz) butter

75ml (3fl oz) milk

125g (4½oz) plain flour

½ tsp ground nutmeg

2 tsp baking powder

2 pears, peeled, cored and sliced

25g (1oz) caster or granulated sugar, for sprinkling

Equipment

900g (2lb) loaf tin

Preheat the oven to 200°C (400°F), Gas mark 6. Line the base and sides of the loaf tin with baking parchment.

Using a hand-held electric beater, whisk the eggs, caster sugar and vanilla extract in a large bowl until the mixture is thick and mousse-like (this will take about 5 minutes).

Melt the butter in a saucepan with the milk, then pour onto the eggs, whisking all the time. Sift in the flour, nutmeg and baking powder and fold carefully into the batter so that there are no lumps of flour. Pour the mixture into the prepared tin and smooth the surface.

Arrange the pear slices over the batter. They will sink to the bottom (this is meant to happen!). Sprinkle with the remaining sugar and bake in the oven for 10 minutes.

Reduce the oven temperature to 180°C (350°F), Gas mark 4, and bake for a further 30–35 minutes or until well risen, golden brown and a skewer inserted into the centre comes out clean.

Allow to sit in the tin for 20 minutes before taking out. Cut into slices to serve.

This takes its name from the traditional Irish Barmbrack, or Bairín Breac, a sweet yeast bread with dried fruit that's served at Halloween. While this version contains no yeast, it is jam packed with lots of lovely dried fruit that will keep it delicious for more than a week

Afternoon fruit brack

SERVES 8

Juice and finely grated zest of 1 orange

25g (1oz) dried apricots, chopped into roughly 5mm (¼in) pieces

25g (1oz) dried cranberries, cut in half

25g (1oz) dried figs, chopped into roughly 5mm (¼in) pieces

25g (1oz) dried dates, chopped into roughly 5mm (¼in) pieces

25g (1oz) crystallised or stem ginger, finely chopped

150g (5oz) caster or granulated sugar

200g (7oz) butter

3 eggs

250g (9oz) plain flour

1 tsp baking powder

Equipment

900g (2lb) loaf tin

Preheat the oven to 180°C (350°F), Gas mark 4. Line the base and sides of the loaf tin with baking parchment.

Pour the juice of the orange into a small saucepan and add all the dried fruit. Place over a medium heat and bring just to the boil, then remove from the heat and transfer to a small bowl to cool.

Place the orange zest in a large bowl with the sugar and butter. Cream together the butter and sugar, then add the eggs one by one, beating all the time. Sift in the flour and baking powder and fold just to mix, then stir in the juice and the fruit.

Transfer the mixture to the prepared loaf tin, place in the oven and bake for about 50 minutes until golden and a skewer inserted into the centre comes out clean.

INDULGENT
& DECADENT

Honey soufflés

Chocolate and hazelnut praline ice cream

Lavender and honey panna cotta

Apple crumble ice cream

Gooey date and stem ginger pudding

Chocolate coconut cake

Layered mocha mousse coffee meringue

American chocolate fudge pie

Honey semifreddo with butter toffee figs

Double chocolate mousse cake

Pistachio and saffron kulfi

Date and almond tart

Date, cardamom and ginger upside-down cake

Drops au chocolat

People seem to think soufflés are extremely difficult to make, but really they are not. It's more about the timing. In this recipe, I show you how to cook them in advance for entertaining, which makes them a deliciously convenient dessert. I adore the contrast of textures and temperatures that you get here, with the cold, creamy Milk ice cream sitting on top of the hot, light, fluffy soufflé.

Honey soufflés

SERVES 4

For the moulds

15g (½oz) butter

25g (1oz) caster sugar

For the soufflés

125ml (4½fl oz) milk

Finely grated zest of 1 small lemon

2 eggs

50g (2oz) honey

1 tbsp cornflour

Pinch of salt

25g (1oz) caster sugar

For the top of the soufflés

15g (½oz) caster sugar

Equipment

4 x 100ml (3½fl oz) capacity soufflé moulds or ovenproof cups

Cont. overleaf

Rub the 15g (½oz) butter around the insides of the soufflé moulds, then dust with the 25g (1oz) sugar. This will create a lovely light crust on the outside of the soufflés. Set aside until later.

Place the milk and the lemon zest in a saucepan on a low–medium heat and bring to the boil, then set aside.

Meanwhile, separate the eggs and place the whites in a mixing bowl and the yolks in another bowl. Into the yolks add the honey, cornflour and salt and whisk until thoroughly mixed. Pour the milk through a sieve and onto the egg yolk mixture, whisking as you pour and making sure it's properly mixed. Pour back into the milk saucepan and place on a medium heat, whisking all the time. It will thicken as it heats up. Don't stop whisking or you'll get a lumpy custard. Once it's thickened and smooth, take it off the heat and transfer into a bowl to cool a little until it's tepid. This may take up to about 10 minutes. Stir it regularly to cool it faster. If there are any lumps, push the custard through a sieve.

When the custard has cooled, you can start whisking the egg whites. Whisk for a minute or two until they turn frothy, then add the caster sugar gradually, whisking all the time until they form stiff peaks. Take a quarter of the egg white mixture and, using a large metal spoon or a spatula, fold it into the custard. When it is thoroughly mixed in, tip the remaining egg white into the custard and fold in very gently, trying not to knock out any air.

Divide the mixture into the four prepared soufflé moulds, making sure you smooth over the tops with a spatula or palette knife. Run your thumb and index finger around the edges to 'clean' the sides. This helps the soufflé to rise evenly. Clean off any mixture that may have dripped onto the sides of the moulds.

The soufflés can now either be baked, stored for later in the fridge for up to 3 hours or stored in the freezer for up to 1 week (cover them with cling film once they're frozen or place them in a plastic storage box).

To bake the soufflés, preheat the oven to 180°C (350°F), Gas mark 4, and place a baking tray in the oven to preheat, too. If using frozen soufflés, remove them from the freezer 1 hour before baking.

Scatter the 15g (½oz) of sugar over the top of the soufflés and bake for 10–15 minutes until they are golden brown on top and have risen 1–2cm (½–¾in) above the tops of the moulds. The baking time will vary depending on the size of the soufflé moulds, but when you gently press the centre of a soufflé with your finger, it should have a very light spring.

Remove from the oven and place on plates. Dust the tops of the soufflés with icing sugar and carefully place a scoop of Milk ice cream (see page 77) on top. Serve immediately.

Rachel's Tip: A baked soufflé waits for nobody, so make sure your guests are sitting at the table before the soufflés are served. This is because the beautiful light soufflés will start to sink 1 or 2 minutes after they come out of the oven!

A no-holds-barred rich chocolate ice cream with crunchy, caramelised hazelnuts swirled throughout. A delicious combination of textures and flavours in one bowl.

Chocolate and hazelnut praline ice cream

SERVES 10–12

For the praline

100g (3½oz) caster or granulated sugar

100g (3½oz) hazelnuts

For the ice cream

600ml (1 pint) double or regular cream

100g (3½oz) caster or granulated sugar

4 egg yolks

1 tsp vanilla extract

150g (5oz) dark chocolate (55–70% cocoa solids)

Equipment

Sugar thermometer (optional)

First, make the praline. Line a baking tray with baking parchment and set aside. Place the sugar in a frying pan and scatter the hazelnuts over the sugar. Place on a medium heat, not stirring but swirling the pan every so often to caramelise the sugar evenly. Cook until the sugar has completely melted and is a deep golden colour. Swirl the pan again so that the hazelnuts are coated in the caramel.

Transfer the coated nuts to the prepared baking tray and allow to cool completely. Once cool, break up the praline using your hands, then place in a food processor and whiz until it resembles coarse breadcrumbs.

Next, make the ice cream. Whisk the cream until it is just holding a soft peak. Place in the fridge until later. Combine the sugar and 200ml (7fl oz) water in a small saucepan, then stir over a medium heat until the sugar is completely dissolved. Remove the spoon and boil the syrup until it reaches the 'thread' stage, 106–113°C (223–235°F). If you don't have a sugar thermometer, the mixture should look thick and syrupy, and when a metal spoon is dipped in, the last drops of syrup will form thin threads.

Meanwhile, place the egg yolks in the bowl of an electric food mixer and whisk until pale and fluffy. When the syrup is at the correct temperature, gradually, and on a slow speed, pour the boiling syrup over the egg yolks, whisking constantly. Once all the syrup is incorporated, turn the speed up to high, add the vanilla extract, and continue to whisk until the mixture is a thick, pale mousse. It will hold a figure of eight.

While you are whisking the egg mousse, place the chocolate in a heatproof bowl over a saucepan of water on a medium heat. Bring the water just up to the boil, then take off the heat and allow the chocolate to melt slowly.

Allow to cool slightly, then add some of the mousse to the chocolate and stir quickly; add more, then combine them together thoroughly. Don't panic if it starts to seize – keep mixing and it will loosen. Now fold in the softly whipped cream. Place in a freezable container, cover and put in the freezer.

After an hour and a half, as the ice cream is just beginning to set, stir in three-quarters of the praline, then return to the freezer to set completely for about 6 hours or overnight. Serve with the remaining praline over the top.

A delicious and elegant dessert to serve on a balmy evening or, indeed, at any time of the year. Lavender, honey and cream are a most delicious combination. This is summer on a plate.

Lavender and honey panna cotta

SERVES 4

10 stalks of lavender (2 tsp buds if already off the stalk)

300ml (½ pint) double or regular cream

40g (1½oz) honey

1 sheet of gelatine

Fresh raspberries or poached peaches (page 96), to serve

Pick the flower buds from the lavender stalks and place in a saucepan with the cream and honey. Place on a medium heat and bring just to the boil, then remove from the heat and allow to infuse for 10 minutes.

Place the gelatine sheet in a bowl of cold water for 3–5 minutes, until softened. Remove the gelatine from its soaking water and squeeze out any excess liquid.

Rewarm the cream mixture and drop in the softened gelatine, stir to dissolve, then strain through a sieve and divide into four serving glasses or little pots. Leave in the fridge to set for about 3 or 4 hours.

Serve with fresh raspberries or poached peaches.

When you think of how delicious a freshly baked apple crumble tastes when it has a scoop of vanilla ice cream slowly melting into it, it's not surprising that this works so well.

Apple crumble ice cream

SERVES 8–10

50g (2oz) butter

50g (2oz) brown sugar

2 eating apples, peeled, cored and cut in to 1cm (½in) chunks

For the ice cream

3 egg yolks

75g (3oz) caster or granulated sugar

1 tsp vanilla extract

800ml (1½ pints) softly whipped cream (measured when whisked)

For the crumble mix

50g (2oz) plain flour

25g (1oz) brown sugar

25g (1oz) rolled (porridge) oats

25g (1oz) butter, cut in to 1cm cubes

Equipment

Sugar thermometer (optional)

To make the ice cream, place the egg yolks in a bowl and whisk until light and fluffy. Combine the sugar and 150ml (5fl oz) water in a small saucepan, then stir over a medium heat until the sugar is completely dissolved. Remove the spoon and boil the syrup until it reaches the 'thread' stage, 106–113°C (223–235°F). If you don't have a sugar thermometer, the mixture should look thick and syrupy, and when a metal spoon is dipped in, the last drops of syrup will form thin threads. Pour this boiling syrup in a steady stream onto the egg yolks, whisking all the time. Add the vanilla extract and continue to whisk until it becomes a thick, creamy white mousse. Fold in the softly whipped cream, place in a container, cover and place in the freezer for an hour.

Next, cook the apples. Place the butter in a pan on a medium heat. When melted, stir in the sugar just until dissolved, then add the apple and cook, stirring occasionally, for about 10 minutes until the apple is soft. Remove from the heat and set aside to cool.

Preheat the oven to 160°C (320°F), Gas mark 3.

To make the crumble, in a bowl, mix together the flour, sugar and rolled oats, then rub in the butter to form a crumbly consistency. Spread out on a piece of baking parchment on a baking tray. Place in an oven and bake for about 15 minutes until golden and crisp, then set aside and allow to cool.

Remove the ice cream from the freezer and mix together the semi-frozen ice cream with the crumble and apple in a bowl, then return to the freezer to freeze all the way through. This should take 3–4 hours.

A real family favourite. The dates bring a rich unctuousness to this pudding, while the ginger stops it from being too sweet and provides a nice little kick. This is completely divine with lots of custard or some softly whipped cream.

Gooey date and stem ginger pudding

SERVES 6

75g (3oz) stoned dates, chopped

75g (3oz) butter

1 egg

250ml (9fl oz) milk

40g (1½oz) stem ginger in syrup

125g (4½oz) plain flour

1½ tsp baking powder

125g (4½oz) dark brown sugar

½ tsp salt

Softly whipped cream or custard, to serve

For the sauce

125g (4½oz) dark brown sugar

150ml (5fl oz) boiling water

50g (2oz) butter

2 tbsp stem ginger syrup from the jar

Equipment

1 litre (1¾ pint) capacity pie dish

Preheat the oven to 180°C (350°F), Gas mark 4.

Place the chopped dates in a small saucepan with the butter over a medium heat and allow the butter to melt, then take off the heat. Whisk the egg in a bowl, then add in the milk, the butter and date mixture. Drain the ginger, reserving the syrup, chop very finely and add to the bowl.

Place the flour, baking powder, brown sugar and salt in a mixing bowl. Mix, then make a well in the centre. Pour in the wet ingredients and stir to combine. Pour into the pie dish.

Next, make the sauce. Place the dark brown sugar, boiling water, butter and ginger syrup in a saucepan on a high heat and bring to the boil, stirring to melt the butter. As soon as it comes to a rolling boil, pour it evenly over the batter in the dish and place in the preheated oven (this may look a little strange, but it will create the beautiful sauce at the bottom). Cook for 40–45 minutes until just set in the centre.

Remove from the oven, allow to cool very slightly, then serve with softly whipped cream or custard.

It's no coincidence that the two primary flavours in this cake are so good together, as this recipe is inspired by what was, and perhaps still is, my very favourite chocolate bar ever! As a treat after church every Sunday, my sister and I were allowed to run down to the local shop to choose a bar, and the chocolate-covered one with the sweet, creamy coconut inside won hands down every time.

Chocolate coconut cake

SERVES 8-10

175g (6oz) butter, softened, plus extra for greasing

300g (11oz) ground almonds

100g (3½oz) desiccated coconut

50g (2oz) cocoa powder

½ tsp salt

1 x 400ml (14fl oz) tin of full-fat coconut milk

75g (3oz) dark chocolate (55–70% cocoa solids)

250g (9oz) caster sugar

3 eggs

For the ganache

200g (7oz) dark chocolate (55–70% cocoa solids)

50ml (2fl oz) Malibu (optional) or a few drops of coconut extract

Equipment

23cm (9in) spring-form cake tin

Cont. overleaf

Preheat the oven to 180°C (350°F), Gas mark 4. Line the base of the tin and grease the sides.

In a bowl combine the almonds, coconut, cocoa powder and salt. Pour half the coconut milk into a saucepan and bring to the boil. Take off the heat and stir in the chocolate until melted, then set aside.

Place the butter in a bowl and beat until soft, then add the sugar and beat for another minute until light and creamy. Add the eggs while beating, one by one. Next, stir in the chocolate and coconut milk mixture and the dry ingredients. Pour into the prepared tin and bake for 40–45 minutes until a skewer inserted into the centre comes out clean. Allow to sit in the tin for 10–20 minutes before taking out (remove the sides, then tip upside down to remove the base and paper). Tip back upright and cool.

While the cake cools, make the chocolate coconut ganache. Place the remaining 200ml (7fl oz) of coconut milk in a saucepan and bring to the boil, then remove from the heat, tip in the chocolate and stir to melt. Add in the Malibu, if using, or a few drops of coconut extract and place in the fridge, stirring every 20 minutes or so, until stiff enough to spread over and around the cooled cake.

Serve scattered with the coconut crumb (see overleaf). This cake keeps really well for days and days.

For the coconut crumb

75g (3oz) caster or granulated sugar

35ml (1fl oz) water

75g (3oz) desiccated coconut

Coconut crumb

Preheat the oven to 180°C (350°F), Gas mark 4. Place a sheet of baking parchment on a baking tray. Place the sugar and water in a saucepan over a medium heat and stir to dissolve the sugar before it comes to the boil. Once the syrup boils, stop stirring and continue to boil for 1 minute. Take off the heat and pour into a bowl with the coconut. Mix thoroughly and spread out evenly over the baking parchment. Bake in the oven for 4–7 minutes until golden. Take out halfway through cooking and mix it up so that it browns evenly, as the coconut around the outside will turn golden first.

Take out of the oven and allow to sit on the tray until cool. Break it up as it cools, then transfer to a jar or bowl. This will keep for 2–3 weeks.

From the fifteenth to the seventeenth centuries, Mocha, the Yemeni port on the Red Sea, was famous for being a major marketplace for coffee. The Mocha coffee beans are known for their distinctive rich chocolate flavour, which gives inspiration to this show-stopping meringue and mousse-layered cake.

Layered mocha mousse coffee meringue

SERVES 10–12

For the meringue

20g (¾oz) freshly ground coffee

250g (9oz) caster sugar

4 egg whites

¼ tsp cream of tartar

For the mocha mousse

100g (3½oz) dark chocolate (55–70% cocoa solids)

20g (¾oz) freshly ground coffee

2 eggs + 1 egg white

Pinch of salt

Cont. overleaf

Preheat the oven to 150°C (300°F), Gas mark 2 (I use a fan oven at 135°C for this). Line two baking trays with baking parchment.

To make the meringue, place the coffee, 3 tablespoons water and 50g (2oz) of the sugar in a small saucepan and bring up to the boil, stirring to dissolve the sugar, then take off the heat and let the coffee infuse.

Place the egg whites in the bowl of an electric food mixer with the whisk attached, add the cream of tartar and whisk until frothy. Add in the remaining caster sugar gradually and continue to whisk until it holds stiff peaks.

Once the egg white mixture is stiff, stop whisking and pour in every bit of the coffee mixture through a sieve. Fold it through carefully, then divide out between the two trays and spread into four ovals, two on each tray, about 20cm (8in) wide and 26cm (10in) long. Make sure the mixture is about 7.5mm (¼in) thick and not too thin around the edges as they can crack and break when cooled.

Place in the oven and cook for 50 minutes, then turn off the oven and allow to cool for at least 1 hour in the oven. If cooking in an Aga, just take them out of the oven and place on top at the side to cool down gently. Once the meringues have cooled, you can assemble the dessert, although stored in an airtight box they will keep for one or two weeks.

For the whipped cream layers

200ml (7fl oz) double or regular cream (measure before whisking)

Cocoa powder, to decorate

Start making the mocha mousse at least 2 hours in advance, so that it can set in the fridge before you assemble the dessert. Place the chocolate in a bowl sitting over a saucepan with a few centimetres of water. Bring the water up to the boil, then take off the heat and allow the chocolate to melt slowly.

Meanwhile, place the coffee and 3 tablespoons water in a small saucepan and bring up to the boil, stir, then remove from the heat and set aside for 5–10 minutes for the coffee to infuse. When the chocolate has melted, pour the coffee through a sieve into the chocolate.

Separate the two eggs and stir the yolks into the chocolate. Whisk all three egg whites with a pinch of salt until stiff, then fold into the chocolate mixture. Place in the fridge to set.

Whip the cream until just stiff, and place in the fridge until you are ready to assemble the meringue.

When ready to assemble, place one meringue oval on your serving plate. Spread over half of the mocha mousse, then top with a second meringue oval. Cover with half the whipped cream, then a third layer of meringue, then cover this with the second half of the mousse, the final meringue and the second half of the cream. Dust with cocoa powder and serve.

Rachel's Tip: For an extra coffee hit you can, if you wish, fold 3 tablespoons of a coffee liqueur through the whipped cream.

If this fudge pie were a person, I reckon it would be Roseanne Barr from the 1980s sitcom Roseanne. *Big, brash and very sweet, this is not for the faint hearted.*

American chocolate fudge pie

SERVES 10–12

For the base

75g (3oz) butter, cut into cubes, plus extra for greasing

115g (4oz) plain flour

25g (1oz) caster sugar

30g (1oz) pecans, chopped quite finely

For the chocolate layer

45g (1½oz) cornflour

30g (1oz) cocoa powder

Pinch of salt

175g (6oz) caster sugar

3 large egg yolks

450ml (16fl oz) milk

25g (1oz) butter

2 tsp vanilla extract

For the creamy layer

250ml (9fl oz) double or regular cream

200g (7oz) cream cheese

150g (5oz) icing sugar

Equipment

23cm (9in) spring-form cake tin

Preheat the oven to 180°C (350°F), Gas mark 4. Butter the sides and the base of the cake tin. Make sure the base is upside down, so that there's no lip and the cake can slide off easily when cooked.

To make the base, place the flour and sugar in a bowl, then rub in the butter until the mixture resembles coarse breadcrumbs. Mix in the pecans, then form a soft dough. Spread evenly into the cake tin.

Place in the oven and bake for 25 minutes until golden. Leave the base in the tin and place on a wire rack to cool.

Meanwhile, make the chocolate layer. Sift the cornflour, cocoa powder and salt into a bowl, then add the sugar and mix well. Beat in the egg yolks and milk and mix together. Transfer to a saucepan, place on a medium heat and cook, whisking continuously, until the mixture boils and becomes very thick. It is at the right thickness when it holds a figure of eight traced into the surface. Whisk in the butter and vanilla extract, then set aside to cool.

Now make the creamy layer. Whisk the cream until quite stiff. Beat the cream cheese and icing sugar to become soft and then fold in the cream.

To assemble, use a dessertspoon to blob all the cream cheese mix onto the biscuit base. Smooth it out a bit, then blob on the chocolate mix. Swirl with the handle of a teaspoon for a marbled effect, then place in the fridge to set. This should take a few hours or could be done overnight.

To serve, unclip the sides of the tin and remove. Using a palette knife or fish slice, slide the cake off the tin base onto a serving plate.

Rachel's Tip: This can be frozen, covered, for 2–3 weeks. It's delicious eaten straight from the freezer.

Literally meaning 'half cold', or 'half frozen', a semifreddo can be anything from a frozen cake to a mousse, but one that does not harden completely in the freezer. This delicious honey-sweetened, almost soft, ice cream is the perfect match for the indulgent and oh-so-good butter toffee figs.

Honey semifreddo with butter toffee figs

SERVES 6–8

For the semifreddo

2 eggs + 2 egg yolks

100g (3½oz) honey

250ml (9fl oz) double or regular cream

For the butter toffee figs

50g (2oz) soft light brown sugar

200g (7oz) fresh figs (about 6–8 figs)

50g (2oz) butter

50g (2oz) honey

50ml (2fl oz) double cream

Equipment

20cm (8in) spring-form cake tin

Line the cake tin with a double layer of cling film.

First, make the semifreddo. Place a saucepan with a few centimetres of water on a medium heat. Put the eggs, egg yolks and honey into a bowl and sit over the saucepan so that the water is not touching the bottom of the bowl. I use a heatproof glass bowl for this (a stainless-steel one is not a good idea, as it will get too hot and scramble the eggs).

Using either a hand whisk or a hand-held electric beater (this is not difficult to do by hand), whisk the eggs and honey over the simmering water for about 5–10 minutes until the mixture is pale, light and will hold a figure of eight. Once it's holding a figure of eight, take the water off the heat and continue to whisk the honey and egg mixture for about 8–10 minutes until it has cooled down to room temperature.

Whip the cream in a mixing bowl until just holding stiff peaks – too stiff and it will go grainy, too soft and it won't be able to hold the honey mousse mixture. Tip one-quarter of the cream into the honey mousse and fold to combine, then tip this mixture into the remaining cream and fold lightly to completely mix, but keeping it light and airy. Tip into the prepared tin, cover with cling film and place in the freezer to freeze.

Cont. overleaf

To make the butter toffee figs, place a frying pan on a medium–high heat and allow to get hot. Scatter the brown sugar on a plate. Cut the figs into wedges from top to bottom, either sixths or eights, depending on the size of the figs. Dip the cut sides of the wedges in the brown sugar so that they're covered with brown sugar (so that it sticks) and put them cut side down into the pan. Allow to caramelise on one cut side before turning to the other cut side.

Once all the figs are cooked and caramelised, take them out, set aside and add the butter, honey and cream to the pan. Stir over the heat and allow to boil for a minute or two until the sauce thickens to a thick butter sauce. Tip the figs back into the pan (this will keep for a few days, just reheat to serve).

When ready to serve, take the semifreddo out of the freezer, remove the cling film, cut into wedges and serve with the warm butter toffee figs over the top, the sauce oozing down the sides.

Rich, flour-free chocolate mousse cake covered with a thick blanket of, yes, rich chocolate mousse. This is a no-holds-barred onslaught of chocolate deliciousness. I recommend using a dark chocolate with somewhere between 55 and 70 per cent in cocoa solids.

Double chocolate mousse cake

SERVES 8–10

For the chocolate mousse cake

50g (2oz) butter, plus extra for greasing

200g (7oz) dark chocolate (55–70% cocoa solids), chopped or in pieces or drops

5 eggs

150g (5oz) caster sugar

Pinch of salt

For the chocolate mousse coating

100g (3½oz) dark chocolate (55–70% cocoa solids)

2 eggs

50g (2oz) butter

Equipment

2 x 18cm (7in) cake tins with 3cm (1¼in) sides

Preheat the oven to 180°C (350°F), Gas mark 4. Line the base of the two cake tins with baking parchment and grease the sides with butter.

To make the mousse cake, place the chocolate and butter in a bowl sitting over a saucepan with a few centimetres of water. Bring the water up to the boil, then take off the heat and allow the chocolate to melt slowly.

Separate the eggs. Place the yolks in a bowl with the sugar and whisk for a few minutes until pale and light. Beat the chocolate mixture into the egg yolk mixture. Whisk the egg whites with the pinch of salt in another bowl until they form stiff peaks, then fold into the chocolate mixture.

Divide the mousse between the two tins and bake in the oven for 30–35 minutes. A skewer inserted into the centre should just come out clean, but remember the mixture should remain moist – it's not a sponge. Take out of the oven and allow to sit for 30 minutes before taking out of the tins.

Next, make the mousse coating. Place the chocolate in a bowl sitting over a saucepan with a few centimetres of water. Bring the water up to the boil, then take off the heat and allow the chocolate to melt slowly.

Separate the eggs and beat the yolks into the warm chocolate, then beat in the butter. Whip the egg whites until stiff peaks form, then fold a quarter into the chocolate mixture, followed by the remainder, which should be folded in gently.

Place in the fridge for 1–2 hours until stiff enough to 'ice' the cake without it falling off. When ready to ice, put one cooled cake upside down on a plate or cake stand. Spread a couple of heaped tablespoons of the mousse over the top as though generously buttering a slice of bread. Cover with the second cake, then ice the top and sides of the cakes.

I remember the very first time I tasted a proper homemade kulfi. It was 1991 and I had just started working in the cookery school at Ballymaloe when Madhur Jaffrey came to teach. I was thrilled to get the opportunity to assist the beautiful, iconic Indian cookery writer. She made this rich Indian ice cream in the traditional way by boiling milk, uncovered, so that it evaporated over time, before adding sugar, nuts and spices. This recipe is close to the version Madhur cooked at Ballymaloe and never fails to bring me back to that lovely day.

Pistachio and saffron kulfi

Serves 6

2 litres (4¼ pints) milk

8 green cardamom pods

½ tsp grated or ground nutmeg

Good pinch of saffron strands

65g (2¼oz) sugar

75g (3oz) pistachios, chopped

Equipment

Ice-cream machine

Moulds (optional)

Place the milk, cardamom pods and nutmeg in a saucepan on a medium heat. Once the milk comes up to a simmer, turn the heat down so that the milk continues to simmer without boiling over. Cook for about 1 hour – the time will vary depending on your pan and the heat, but the milk has to reduce to one-third of its original amount (about 675ml/1¼ pints). Keep stirring regularly as it cooks. It browns a little on the bottom of the saucepan, so don't scrape this bit into the milk.

Pour through a sieve into another saucepan, add the saffron, sugar and half of the chopped pistachios and cook for 2 minutes more. Pour out into a bowl and allow to cool.

Pour into an ice-cream machine or cover and place the bowl (if not using an ice-cream machine) in the freezer. Take out of the freezer after about 2 hours and stir vigorously, then cover and put back into the freezer. Take out again another 2–3 hours later and repeat.

When the kulfi is nearly frozen you can, if you wish, transfer it to individual moulds, then pop back in the freezer overnight, or for at least a couple of hours, until frozen.

Turn out the kulfi and scatter with the remaining pistachios. This is wonderful served just as it is, or with some chopped or sliced ripe mango.

I always think that dates don't quite taste as they look. Brown, a bit wrinkly, not necessarily appetising, but one bite into the sweet, chewy, almost toffee-like dried fruit and it's hard to stop. A favourite since the Garden of Eden, dates really are the food of the gods and have the nutritional benefits to match. They absolutely love being paired with almonds, a match that's showcased to perfection in this rich, decadent tart. Good, plump dates works best for this tart, especially the Medjool date, which comes from Morocco originally and, in my opinion, is the king of dates.

Date and almond tart

SERVES 6–8

For the pastry

200g (7oz) plain flour

1 tbsp icing sugar

Pinch of salt

100g (3½oz) chilled butter, diced

1 egg, beaten

For the frangipane filling

100g (3½oz) butter

100g (3½oz) caster sugar

2 eggs

125g (4½oz) ground almonds

10–12 Medjool dates or 16–20 smaller ones (such as deglet nour), stoned and halved

Cont. overleaf

Sift the flour, icing sugar and salt into a bowl and rub in the butter until the mixture resembles coarse breadcrumbs. Add half the beaten egg and, using your hands, bring the dough together, adding a little more egg if it is too dry.

If you are making the pastry in a food processor, sift in the flour, icing sugar and salt and add the butter. Whiz for a few seconds, then add half the beaten egg and continue to whiz for just a few more seconds until it comes together. You might need to add a little more egg, but don't add too much – it should just come together. Don't over-process the pastry or it will be tough and heavy. Reserve the remaining beaten egg for brushing over the finished pastry.

Without kneading the dough, carefully shape it into a 1–2cm (½–¾in) thick round, using your hands to flatten it. Cover with cling film and place in the fridge to chill for about 30 minutes.

Meanwhile, preheat the oven to 180°C (350°F), Gas mark 4.

Take the pastry out of the fridge and place it between two sheets of cling film (each bigger than your tart tin). Using a rolling pin, roll out the pastry to about 3mm (⅛in) thick. Make sure to keep it in a round shape and large enough to line the base and sides of the tin.

For the apricot glaze

50g (2oz) apricot jam

Juice of ⅛ lemon

Equipment

23cm (9in) loose-bottomed tart tin

Removing just the top layer of cling film, place the pastry upside down (cling-film side facing up) in the tart tin (there's no need to flour or grease the tin). Press the pastry into the edges of the tin, with the cling film still attached to the dough, and using your thumb 'cut' the pastry along the edge of the tin for a neat finish. If there are any holes or gaps in the pastry, simply patch them up with some of your spare pieces of dough.

Remove the cling film and chill the pastry in the fridge for 15 minutes or in the freezer for 5 minutes.

Remove the pastry from the fridge or freezer and line with greaseproof paper or baking parchment, leaving plenty of paper to come up over the sides. Fill the lined tart case with baking beans or dried pulses (you can use these over and over again), and bake 'blind' for 20–25 minutes or until the pastry feels just dry to the touch on the base.

Remove the paper and beans, brush with a little of the remaining beaten egg and return to the oven for 3 minutes. Again, if there are any little holes or cracks in the pastry, patch them up with any leftover raw pastry so that the filling doesn't leak out during cooking. Once the pastry has been baked blind, take it out of the oven and set it aside in the tin.

Next, make the frangipane filling. Cream the butter, gradually beat in the sugar and continue beating until the mixture is light and soft. Gradually add the eggs, beating well. Stir in the ground almonds until just mixed, then pour the frangipane into the pastry case, spreading it evenly. Arrange the dates on top of the frangipane in concentric circles. Bake for 30–35 minutes until golden and just set in the centre.

Meanwhile, to make the apricot glaze, pour the jam and lemon juice into a saucepan and put on a medium heat. Stir together well, then remove from the heat and push the mixture through a sieve. The glaze can be stored in an airtight jar and reheated to melt it before using.

When the tart is cooked, remove it from the oven and brush generously with the apricot glaze while warm.

I'm such a fan of upside-down cakes. I think there is a recipe for at least one in every book of mine. This particular cake has a few of my favourite ingredients: toffee-like dates, warming ginger and its close relative, the cardamom pod. An easy-to-throw-together cake, but still deliciously rich and indulgent.

Date, cardamom and ginger upside-down cake

SERVES 6–8

75g (3oz) butter

200g (7oz) (stoned weight) lovely plump dates (such as Medjool dates), coarsely chopped

75g (3oz) brown sugar

50g (2oz) stem ginger in syrup, finely chopped

3 tbsp stem ginger syrup from the jar

For the cake batter

150g (5oz) butter, cut into cubes

175g (6oz) caster sugar

200g (7oz) plain flour

1 tsp baking powder

1 tsp ground cardamom

3 eggs

Equipment

25cm (10in) ovenproof frying pan

Preheat the oven to 170°C (325°F), Gas mark 3.

Place an ovenproof frying pan over a medium heat and allow to warm up. Add in the butter, allow to melt, then tip in the dates, brown sugar, ginger and the syrup. Stir together and allow to bubble for just about 1 minute until slightly thickened, but don't let it darken. Take off the heat, set aside and make the cake batter.

In the bowl of a food processor, place the butter, sugar, flour, baking powder and ground cardamom. Pulse a few times to mix, then add in the eggs and whiz until it forms a soft dough. Alternatively, place the butter in a bowl and beat until soft, then add in the sugar and beat again; next add the eggs one at a time, and lastly stir in the dry ingredients.

Place tablespoonful blobs of the cake batter over the sticky date mixture in the ovenproof frying pan, carefully spreading to cover, but trying not to disturb the dates, and place in the oven.

Bake for 25–30 minutes until a skewer inserted into the centre comes out clean. Once out of the oven, allow it to sit for just 2 minutes before placing an upturned plate over the pan and flipping out upside down.

A nifty little French recipe for using up scraps of puff pastry, these are heavenly little swirls of buttery, chocolaty deliciousness.

Drops au chocolat

MAKES 12 DROPS

350g (12oz) puff pastry

A little icing sugar, for rolling out

75g (3oz) dark chocolate (55–70% cocoa solids) chopped, or dark chocolate chips or drops

Preheat the oven to 220°C (425°F), Gas mark 7.

Roll the pastry out into a 20 x 30cm (8 x 12in) rectangle, using icing sugar to dust the worktop and the top of the pastry.

Sprinkle the chocolate chips evenly over the whole sheet then, with the long end closest to you, roll up tightly into a log. Place in the fridge to chill for 15 minutes. When chilled, cut into twelve even slices. Place on a baking tray lined with baking parchment and bake for 10–12 minutes until puffed up and golden brown around the edges. Transfer to a wire rack to cool.

CLASSICS
WITH A TWIST

Cinnamon custard tarts

Puff pastry

Rhubarb meringue pie

Salted caramel crème brûlée

Raspberry and white chocolate meringue roulade

Apricot fool with cardamom shortbread fingers

Meringues with pink grapefruit curd and cream

Blueberry bread and butter pudding

Apple and cinnamon baked cheesecake

Strawberry Victoria mess

Pear and maple crumble

Nectarine custard tarts

Orange caramel choux puffs

My agent sometimes calls with strange requests – not strange in a weird way, but just slightly different to the average magazine article or food festival gig. One day she called and said, 'Fancy going to Lisbon for the day and eating Portuguese custard tarts for a TV crew?' Well, no one needs to ask me twice to, number one, go to a beautiful city for the day and, number two, eat custard tarts. So off I went to check out the iconic Portuguese custard tarts, and eat them I did. Nearly every single one of them. This recipe is inspired by those classic Portuguese tarts.

Cinnamon custard tarts

MAKES 12 TARTS

375g (13oz) puff pastry (see page 206), rolled out to 3mm (⅛in) thick and placed in the fridge to chill

Icing sugar, to decorate

For the cinnamon custard

20g (¾oz) plain flour

350ml (12fl oz) milk

225g (8oz) caster sugar

¼ tsp ground cinnamon

5 egg yolks

Equipment

12-hole bun tray (smaller than a cupcake or muffin tray)

Preheat the oven to 230°C (450°F), Gas mark 8.

Make the cinnamon custard. Place the flour, 50ml (2fl oz) of the milk, the caster sugar, cinnamon and the egg yolks in a bowl and whisk for 10 seconds.

Place the remaining 300ml (½ pint) milk in a saucepan and bring to the boil. Pour onto the egg yolk mixture, whisking all the time, and continue to whisk until thoroughly mixed. Pour back into the saucepan, place on a medium heat and stir all the time until it thickens – it needs to boil for 2 minutes. I use a wooden spatula for this, but if it goes lumpy you can use a whisk. Take off the heat.

Take the pastry out of the fridge and cut into twelve 9cm (3½in) discs. Take the bun tray and press the discs into the cups. Divide the custard out among the cups and bake for 8–12 minutes until the pastry is golden. Allow to cool and dust with icing sugar to serve.

Puff pastry takes a little time and effort to perfect, but it's worth having a go and the results are so delicious. If you're pressed for time, you can buy puff pastry from supermarkets – though look for one that contains butter and no oils. This recipe makes generous quantities, so you can store any leftover pastry in the fridge for 48 hours or in the freezer for up to three months.

Puff pastry

MAKES APPROXIMATELY 1.15KG (2½LB)

450g (1lb) strong white flour

Pinch of salt

1 tbsp freshly squeezed lemon juice

200–275ml cold water (the amount of water will depend on the absorbency of the flour)

450g chilled butter, still in its wrapper

Step 1: Sift the flour and salt into a large bowl. Mix the lemon juice with 200ml (7fl oz) water, pour into the flour and, using your hands, mix to a soft but not sticky dough, adding more water if necessary. This dough is called détrempe (a mixture of flour and water). Flatten it slightly and cover with a plastic bag, cling film or greaseproof paper and allow to rest in the fridge on a baking tray (which aids the chilling process) for 30 minutes.

Step 2: Roll the détrempe into a rectangle about 1cm (½in) thick. Remove the butter from the fridge, still in its wrapper and, using a rolling pin, 'beat' it until it forms a slab about 1.5–2cm (⅝–¾in) thick. Remove the wrapper, place the butter in the centre of the dough rectangle and fold the dough over the edges of the butter to make a neat parcel, covering the butter.

Step 3: Turn the dough over and, dusting the work surface with flour to stop the dough from sticking, roll it gently out into a rectangle approximately 40cm (16in) long and 20cm (8in) wide, positioned so that one narrow end is facing you. Brush off the excess flour with a pastry brush, then fold neatly into three by lifting the end furthest away from you and placing it on the rectangle, so that only one-third of the pastry is left uncovered, and aligning the sides as accurately as possible. Fold the other end on top. Seal the edges with your hands or a rolling pin.

Step 4: Give the dough a one-quarter turn (90 degrees), so that the folds are running vertically in front of you (it should look like a closed book) Roll out away from you, again into a rectangle (to roughly the same measurements as before), brush off any excess flour and fold in three again. Seal the edges, cover with cling film or greaseproof paper and allow to rest in the fridge for another 30 minutes.

Repeat steps 3 and 4 twice more (always ensuring that you start the process with the folds in the pastry running vertically, i.e. looking like a closed book), so that in the end the dough has been rolled out six times and has rested in the fridge three times for 30 minutes each time.

Chill for at least 1 hour before using.

One of my fail-safe Sunday lunch puddings is poached rhubarb with meringues and cream. Tart rhubarb is the ideal foil for sugary meringues, and whipped cream perfectly bridges the gap between them. This recipe is a delightful amalgamation of this and another classic: lemon meringue pie. Use the pinkest rhubarb you can for a pretty pink curd.

Rhubarb meringue pie

SERVES 6

For the sweet shortcrust pastry

200g (7oz) plain flour

Pinch of salt

100g (3½oz) butter

25g (1oz) icing sugar

1 egg, beaten

For the rhubarb curd

550g (1lb 3oz) rhubarb, cut in to 1cm (½in) slices (weigh when sliced and trimmed)

200g (7oz) caster or granulated sugar

75g (3oz) butter

3 eggs, whisked

Cont. overleaf

First, make the sweet shortcrust pastry. Place the flour, salt, butter and icing sugar in a food processor and whiz briefly until the butter is in small lumps. Add half the beaten egg and continue to whiz for just another few seconds until the mixture looks as though it may come together when pressed (prolonged processing will only toughen the pastry, so don't whiz it up until it is a ball of dough). You might need to add a little more egg, but not too much as the mixture should be just moist enough to come together.

If making by hand, rub the butter into the flour, salt and icing sugar until the mixture resembles coarse breadcrumbs then, using your hands, add just enough beaten egg to bring it together.

With your hands, flatten out the ball of dough until it is about 2cm (¾in) thick, then wrap in cling film or place in a plastic bag and leave in the fridge for at least 30 minutes.

Preheat the oven to 180°C (350°F), Gas mark 4.

Remove the pastry from the fridge and place between two sheets of cling film (each bigger than your tart tin). Using a rolling pin, roll the pastry out to no thicker than 5mm (¼in). If the tin is round, keep the pastry in a round shape and make sure it is large enough to line both the base and the sides of the tin.

Remove the top layer of cling film, place your hand, palm facing up, under the cling film underneath, then flip the pastry over, cling-film side facing up, and into the tart tin. Press the pastry into the edges of the tin, with the cling film still attached to the pastry, and, using your thumb, 'cut' the pastry along

For the meringue

4 egg whites (about 150–170g/5–6oz)

110g (4oz) caster sugar

110g (4oz) icing sugar

Equipment

23cm (9in) loose-bottomed flan ring or tart tin

the edge of the tin for a neat finish. Remove the cling film and, if you have time, chill the pastry in the fridge for another 30 minutes or in the freezer for 10 minutes (it can keep for weeks like this, covered, in the freezer). If the pastry has remained cold while rolling it out, there is no need to chill it again.

Next, line the pastry with baking parchment, leaving plenty to come up the sides. Fill with baking beans or dried pulses (all of which can be reused again and again). Place in the oven and bake 'blind' for 20–25 minutes until the pastry feels dry on the base. Remove from the oven, take out the baking beans and paper and brush the base of the pastry with any leftover beaten egg, then cook in the oven for another 3 minutes. When completely blind baked, take out of the oven and set the pastry aside. Turn the oven down to 150°C (300°F), Gas mark 2.

Next, make the curd. Place the rhubarb and 50g (2oz) of the sugar in a saucepan over a medium heat and cook for about 5–6 minutes, stirring every so often, until the rhubarb has softened, broken up completely and the mixture has thickened to a pulp.

Pour into a sieve sitting over a bowl and push the mixture through the sieve into the bowl, making sure to scrape the underside of the sieve to get every last bit.

Next, place the butter in the cleaned saucepan on a low–medium heat and allow to melt. Take off the heat just while you add in the eggs, the remaining sugar and the rhubarb purée. Put back on a low heat and stir continuously for about 6–8 minutes until thickened. Take off the heat, tip into a bowl and allow to cool.

Place the egg whites for the meringue in the bowl of an electric food mixer with the whisk attachment (or use a hand-held electric beater). Whisk at full speed for a few minutes until the egg whites hold fluffy, stiff peaks when the whisk is lifted.

Continue whisking and add the caster sugar one tablespoon at a time, but with a few seconds between each addition. Once all the caster sugar is added in, stop the whisk. Sift in one-third of the icing sugar and fold in carefully, using a spatula, then fold in the second third, and finally the last third. The mixture should be fluffy and light.

Spread the curd all over the tart base, then tip the meringue on top, making peaks with the back of a spoon. Place the tart in the oven and bake for 35–45 minutes until the meringue topping is crisp and lightly browned on the outside.

Take out of the oven and allow to sit in the tin for 5 minutes before removing from the tin. I do this by sitting the tin on a small bowl and allowing the sides to fall down, then carefully sliding the shortcrust pastry crust off the base of the tin, using something flat like a palette knife. Allow to cool before cutting into slices to serve.

The English, French and the Spanish all like to think that they originally created the crème brûlée, and indeed each country has recorded versions of the recipe dating as far back as the 1600s. Whoever was the initial instigator of the burnt-sugar-topped custard pudding we cannot be exactly sure, but what is certain is that crème brûlée loves to take on other flavours, and this salted caramel variation works a treat.

Salted caramel crème brûlée

SERVES 4

For the custards

50g (2oz) caster or granulated sugar

250ml (9fl oz) double or regular cream

⅛ tsp salt

2 egg yolks

For the caramel topping

100g (3½oz) caster or granulated sugar

Few pinches of sea salt flakes, such as Irish Atlantic Sea Salt, Oriel, Maldon or Halen Môn

First make the custards. Place the sugar in a small saucepan on a medium heat and leave for a few minutes. When the sugar starts to caramelise around the edge of the pan, give it a shake and swirl and return to the heat. Repeat once or twice more until it is all caramelised with no sugar left. It will be smoking and a deep golden brown when ready. Too light and you won't get the deep caramel flavour. Too dark and it'll taste bitter. Immediately pour in the cream and the salt, then turn the heat down to low and allow the caramel to dissolve completely in the cream. Set aside off the heat.

Place the egg yolks in a bowl and pour over the warm caramel, whisking all the time. Pour this back into the saucepan and stir over a low heat, using a flat-bottomed wooden spoon (to get into the edges) until the mixture coats the back of it. You need to be careful – if it gets too hot it will scramble; you might need to take it off the heat every so often if it starts to catch. As soon as it's ready, and while still hot, pour the mixture into four cups or bowls and set aside. You need to allow a 'skin' to develop on each custard, so do not shake them or cover them while warm. When cool, place in the fridge to set.

Next day, take the custards out of the fridge. Place the 100g (3½oz) of sugar in a saucepan and caramelise as before. Spoon it over the custards, then immediately sprinkle a tiny pinch of salt flakes over each before the caramel hardens. Allow to sit for 5 minutes before serving.

Rachel's Tip: If you have a blowtorch, instead of making caramel, scatter over the custards a 2mm (⅛in) layer of caster or granulated sugar. Wave the blowtorch slowly over the sugar, from about 10cm (4in) away, until it is deep golden and caramelised. Allow to sit for 5 minutes before serving.

Coming from the French verb *rouler*, meaning 'to roll', a roulade can be applied to anything, be it a slice of meat or a thick sheet of soft marshmallow meringue. Though ever so slightly 1980s, a roulade never fails to please, and I particularly love this version with raspberries and white chocolate.

Raspberry and white chocolate meringue roulade

SERVES 6–8

For the coulis

Juice of ½ lemon

100g (3½oz) raspberries, fresh or frozen

1–2 tbsp icing sugar

For the meringue

50g (2oz) hazelnuts

4 large egg whites

200g (7oz) caster sugar

1 tsp cornflour

1 tsp vinegar (such as white wine vinegar) or lemon juice

Cont. overleaf

First, make the coulis. Place the ingredients in a food processor or blender, whiz for a few minutes until smooth, then pour through a sieve into a bowl.

Preheat the oven to 160°C (320°F), Gas mark 3.

Place the hazelnuts on a baking tray and toast in the oven for 5–6 minutes until golden, then remove from the oven. Tip into a tea towel and rub to loosen the skins. Pick out the nuts from the skins, then roughly chop.

Next, line the Swiss roll tin with an oiled piece of foil so that there's enough to come up the sides by about 4cm (1½in), as the meringue will rise as it cooks.

Using a hand-held electric beater or food mixer, whisk the egg whites until almost stiff, then pour in (while still whisking) the sugar gradually and whisk until stiff. Add in the cornflour and vinegar or lemon juice, then whisk again just for a few seconds until mixed. Lastly, fold in the chopped, toasted hazelnuts.

Spread out in the lined tray and bake for 18–20 minutes until light golden and softly springy in the centre. Take out of the oven and let sit for about 5 minutes before turning out onto another sheet of foil. Allow to cool completely.

For the filling

100g (3½oz) white chocolate, broken into pieces or drops

200ml (7fl oz) double or regular cream

1 tsp vanilla extract

150g (5oz) fresh raspberries

Equipment

23 x 37cm (9 x 15in) Swiss roll tin

Place the white chocolate in a bowl sitting over a saucepan with a few centimetres of water. Bring the water up to the boil, then take off the heat and allow the chocolate to melt slowly over the water (I find this is the best way to melt white chocolate to prevent it 'blocking'). Once the chocolate has melted, take the bowl off the saucepan and allow to cool.

Meanwhile, whip the cream – but stop whisking just before it reaches the stiff-peak stage. Once the white chocolate has cooled, fold it into the cream with the vanilla extract, then spread out to cover the surface of the meringue. Scatter with raspberries.

With the larger end of the meringue facing you (and using the foil to help) roll the meringue away from you to form a roulade. Turn out onto a plate (with the join underneath) and serve with the raspberry coulis.

Cardamom and apricot have long been paired together in everything from Danish pastries to jams, and this great little match continues to work its magic in a fluffy light fool with crumbly shortbread fingers.

Apricot fool with cardamom shortbread fingers

SERVES 6

For the fool

6 large fresh ripe apricots (about 450g/1lb with stones)

125g (4½oz) caster or granulated sugar

200ml (7fl oz) double or regular cream (measured before whisking)

For the cardamom shortbread fingers

150g (5oz) plain flour

50g (2oz) caster sugar

½ tsp freshly ground cardamom seeds (from about 16 green cardamom pods)

100g (3½oz) butter, cubed

Cut the apricots in half and remove the stones. Place in a saucepan with the sugar and 2 tablespoons water over a medium heat. Stir to dissolve the sugar, then cook, covered, for 10–15 minutes until the apricots are completely soft. If there is any liquid in the bottom of the pan, continue to cook, uncovered, to allow it to evaporate until the juices are thick. Place in a blender and whiz, then allow to cool. The mixture should be quite a thick purée. If it's not thick enough, put it back on the heat and cook, uncovered, and stirring regularly, until it's a bit thicker. If it's too liquidy, the fool will not be fluffy. Remove from the heat and allow to cool completely.

While it's cooling, you can whisk the cream until not quite, but almost, stiff. Fold the cream into the apricot purée. Store in the fridge until ready to serve.

Preheat the oven to 180°C (350°F), Gas mark 4.

To make the cardamom shortbread fingers, place the flour in a bowl with the sugar and the cardamom and mix, then rub in the butter and squeeze in your hands to bring it together to form a dough. Alternatively, you could bring the ingredients together very briefly in a food processor.

Roll the dough out until 5mm (¼in) thick, keeping it in a square or a rectangle. Pierce it all over with a skewer or fork, then cut it into twelve fingers about 10 x 2cm (4 x ¾in) in size.

Place on a baking tray (no need to grease or line) and bake for 5–8 minutes until light golden. Take out and let stand on the tray for 2 minutes before transferring to a wire rack.

Serve the shortbread fingers with the apricot fool.

I love experimenting with different-flavoured curds and the unique balance of the pink grapefruit's sweetness and tang is ideal for accompanying meringues and cream. The meringue recipe works a treat: half caster and half icing sugar, with a hint of vanilla for flavour, these are generous, big cushions of fluffy sweetness.

Meringues with pink grapefruit curd and cream

MAKES 10 MERINGUES

For the meringues

4 egg whites

110g (4oz) caster sugar

110g (4oz) icing sugar

1 tsp vanilla extract

250ml (9fl oz) double or regular cream

For the grapefruit curd

75g (3oz) butter

Juice and finely grated zest of 1 pink grapefruit

75g (3oz) caster or granulated sugar

2 eggs + 1 egg yolk

Preheat the oven to 110°C (225°F), Gas mark ¼ (or use a fan oven at 100°C for this).

Line two baking trays with baking parchment. Place the egg whites in the bowl of an electric food mixer with the whisk attachment (or use a hand-held electric beater). Whisk at full speed for a few minutes until the egg whites hold fluffy, stiff peaks when the whisk is lifted.

Continue whisking and add the caster sugar one tablespoon at a time, but with a few seconds between each addition. Once all the caster sugar is added in, stop the whisk. Sift in one-third of the icing sugar and fold in carefully, using a spatula, then fold in the second third and finally the last third and the vanilla extract. The mixture should be fluffy and light.

Scoop a heaped tablespoonful of the mixture onto a baking tray, using a second tablespoon to help ease it off, to form blobs (or if you prefer, make a little dip or well in the centre to hold the whipped cream and curd). Repeat with all the mixture, place in the oven and cook for 1½ hours until the meringues are crisp on the outside and will lift off the baking parchment.

Place the butter in a saucepan on a medium–low heat and when melted, whisk in the juice, zest, sugar, eggs and egg yolk. Turn the heat down to low and cook, stirring constantly, until thick enough to coat the back of a spoon. Then remove from the heat and allow to cool.

Softly whisk the cream, then place generous blobs on the meringues and drizzle with the grapefruit curd.

A bread and butter pudding is a classic – and for good reason, too. White bread soaked in sweet vanilla-scented custard and baked in the oven, what's not to love? There are countless variations on the theme and this is one of my favourites. Use fresh or frozen blueberries.

Blueberry bread and butter pudding

SERVES 6–8

50g (2oz) butter, softened, plus extra for greasing

12 slices of good-quality bread, crusts removed

250g (9oz) blueberries

675ml (1¼ pints) double or regular cream

325ml (11fl oz) milk

6 eggs

225g (8oz) caster sugar

2 tsp vanilla extract

2 tbsp granulated sugar

Softly whipped cream, to serve

Equipment

2 litre (4 pint) capacity gratin dish

Preheat the oven to 180°C (350°F), Gas mark 4. Rub the bottom and sides of a gratin dish with butter.

Butter the bread slices on one side. Arrange a single layer of bread in the gratin dish, butter side up. Scatter a good handful of blueberries over the layer, then use more bread to make another layer in the dish. Scatter another handful of blueberries over this layer, then make another layer of bread. Continue in this way until you have used all of your bread and blueberries. I like to have neat, overlapping triangles of bread on the top layer.

Place the cream and milk in a saucepan and bring to just under the boil.

While it's heating up, in a separate bowl whisk the eggs, caster sugar and vanilla extract, then pour the hot milk and cream into the eggs and whisk to combine. Pour this custard over the bread and leave to soak for 10 minutes.

Sprinkle the granulated sugar over the top, then prepare a bain-marie. Place the gratin dish in a large, deep-sided roasting tin and pour in enough boiling water to come about halfway up the sides of the dish. This regulates the heat in the oven and ensures that the eggs don't scramble.

Carefully transfer the dish and bain-marie to the oven and cook for 1 hour. The top should be golden and the centre should be just set. Serve with softly whipped cream.

Part Bavarian, part American, this is equally as good enjoyed at the end of a meal as with a cup of coffee. The ginger nut biscuits bring a lovely warmth to the cheesecake base, but feel free to use whichever type of biscuit you like. Make sure you just cook the cheesecake until it has a thick wobble. If it cooks for too long, it will crack all over, which is not the end of the world, but not exactly what you're looking for!

Apple and cinnamon baked cheesecake

SERVES 8

200g (7oz) caster sugar

3 eating apples, peeled, quartered and cores removed

75g (3oz) butter, melted, plus extra for greasing

175g (6oz) ginger nut biscuits

450g (1lb) cream cheese

1 tsp ground cinnamon

4 eggs, lightly beaten

Equipment

24cm (9½in) spring-form cake tin

Place 50g (2oz) of the sugar and 2 tablespoons water in a saucepan and dissolve the sugar over a medium heat. Arrange the apples in the saucepan cut side down and cover with a cartouche (a circle of baking parchment) and a lid. Cook for 2 minutes – there should be a couple of tablespoons of liquid; if there is more, remove the apples and boil to reduce. Take off the heat and leave for 5 minutes with the lid on. Remove the lid and cool.

Preheat the oven to 180°C (350°F), Gas mark 4. Butter the sides and base of the cake tin. Make sure the base is upside down, so that there is no lip and the cake can slide off easily when cooked.

Place the biscuits in a food processor and whiz until quite fine, or place them in a plastic bag and bash with a rolling pin. Mix the crushed biscuits with the melted butter and evenly press them into the base of the tin. Arrange the apple mixture on top and chill in the fridge while you make the topping.

Beat the cream cheese, remaining sugar, cinnamon, eggs and cooking juices together in a large bowl until smooth and creamy. Pour over the top of the apple, then bake in the oven for 40 minutes or until it is set around the outside but still has a wobble in the centre.

Allow to cool completely, then run a knife around the edge to loosen it and carefully remove the cheesecake from the tin by sliding it off the base using a palette knife or fish slice. Transfer to a serving plate. Cut into slices to serve. This cheesecake is best eaten when it is at room temperature.

A simple little twist on the classic Eton mess, but instead of using meringues, this recipe uses Victoria sponge. A delicious quick recipe to assemble on a summer's day.

Strawberry Victoria mess

SERVES 6-8

For the sponge

100g (3½oz) butter, plus extra for greasing

100g (3½oz) plain flour, plus extra for dusting

100g (3½oz) caster or granulated sugar

2 eggs

¾ tsp baking powder

1 tbsp milk

For the strawberries

450g (7oz) strawberries, dehulled

100g (3½oz) caster or granulated sugar, plus 1 tbsp for the purée

Juice of 2 lemons

250ml (9fl oz) double or regular cream

Few sprigs of mint, to decorate

Equipment

1 x 18cm (7in) sandwich tin with 3cm (1¼in) sides

Preheat the oven to 180°C (350°F), Gas mark 4, then butter and flour the sides of the tin and line the base with a disc of baking parchment.

Cream the butter until soft in a large bowl or in an electric food mixer. Add the sugar and beat until the mixture is light and fluffy.

Whisk the eggs in a small bowl for a few seconds until just mixed, then gradually add them to the butter mixture, beating all the time. Sift in the flour and baking powder, then add the milk and fold in gently to incorporate.

Tip the mixture into the tin and place in the centre of the oven. Bake for 18–25 minutes or until golden on top and springy to the touch.

Remove from the oven and allow to cool in the tin for 10 minutes, then loosen around the edges of the cake using a small, sharp knife and carefully remove from the tin. Leave on a wire rack to cool down completely.

Take 100g (3½oz) of the strawberries and place in a food processor with 1 tablespoon of the sugar and the juice of ½ lemon. Whiz for a few minutes, then push through a sieve and set aside.

Slice the remaining strawberries and mix together in a bowl with the 100g (3½oz) of sugar and the remaining lemon juice. Set aside and allow to sit for about an hour or so to become juicy.

Strain off the juices and place in a bowl. Next, cut the sponge in to 1–1.5cm (½–⅝in) pieces and add to the bowl. Mix together well to make sure each sponge piece is moistened.

In a bowl, whisk the cream.

To serve, add in layers to serving glasses first a few pieces of sponge, then some sliced strawberries, a spoonful of cream and finish with a drizzle of the puréed strawberries and a sprig of mint.

This is a decidedly autumnal treat, perfect for enjoying at the end of a long, lazy Sunday lunch. For a deliciously crunchy crumble, make sure to just rub the butter into the flour and sugar so that it's still coarse.

Pear and maple crumble

SERVES 6–8

8 small pears (about 800g), peeled, cored and cut into 1.5cm (⅝in) chunks

50g (2oz) caster or granulated sugar

120ml (4fl oz) maple syrup

For the crumble

100g (3½oz) caster or granulated sugar

150g (5oz) plain flour

75g (3oz) butter, cubed

Equipment

1 litre (1¾ pint) capacity pie dish

Preheat the oven to 180°C (350°F), Gas mark 4.

Place the cut pears in the pie dish, then sprinkle over the sugar and pour over the maple syrup.

In a bowl, mix together the sugar and flour, then rub in the cubes of butter until the mixture looks like coarse breadcrumbs.

Tip the crumble mix over the fruit, then place in the oven and bake for about 30 minutes until the crumble mixture is golden brown. Remove from the oven and allow to cool slightly before serving with softly whipped cream or vanilla ice cream.

Light, buttery puff pastry sitting under vanilla-scented custard and topped with juicy, almost caramelised nectarine slices – divine. This recipe also works very well with apricots, peaches, apples, bananas or rhubarb.

Nectarine custard tarts

MAKES 6 TARTS

For the custard

175ml (6fl oz) milk

100ml (3½fl oz) double or regular cream

½ vanilla pod, split down one side, or 1 tsp vanilla extract

2 egg yolks

50g (2oz) caster sugar

2 tbsp plain flour

375g (13oz) puff pastry (all butter or homemade)

3 ripe nectarines, halved, stones removed and each half sliced into 6 wedges

2 tbsp caster or granulated sugar

First, make the custard. Place the milk, cream and the vanilla pod, if using, in a saucepan and bring to the boil. Set aside to infuse for 5–10 minutes.

Meanwhile, using a hand-held electric beater, whisk together the egg yolks, sugar and flour until pale in colour and thick. Reheat the milk and cream, removing the vanilla pod (this can be wiped clean and reused another time), then pour, while whisking, onto the egg yolk mixture.

Tip back into the saucepan (with the vanilla extract, if using), and stir over a low–medium heat for a few minutes, stirring all the time with a wooden spatula, until thickened (you can use a whisk if it gets lumpy). It will need to boil for about 2 minutes to really thicken. It should coat the back of a spoon. Take out of the saucepan, put into a bowl (or onto a plate if you need to cool quickly) and allow to cool.

Preheat the oven to 220°C (425°F), Gas mark 7. Roll the pastry out on a floured worktop until just 4–5mm (¼in) thick. Trim the edges with a knife, then cut into six rectangles or squares.

Turn each one upside down (so that the cut edges are now cut upwards, which will encourage the pastry edges to rise well), then score (about halfway down through the pastry) a 1cm (½in) border around each (like a picture frame, this will rise and hold in the custard).

Leaving the borders free, spread out a generous heaped tablespoon or two of custard to thickly cover the pastry, then arrange the nectarine slices over the top and sprinkle each pastry with the sugar. Bake for 20 minutes until the pastry is puffed up and golden.

Rachel's Tip: The puff pastry trimmings can be used for the Cinnamon cigars (page 104) or the Drops au chocolat (page 198).

Admittedly one of the more involved recipes in the book, but also one of the most delicious things to eat. Ever. Thin, crisp, burnt sugar caramel coating light choux pastry stuffed with creamy orange-scented custard; these are a real treat.

Orange caramel choux puffs

SERVES 8–10

For the choux pastry

100g (3½oz) strong white or plain flour

Pinch of salt

75g (3oz) butter

3 eggs, beaten

For the crème pâtissière (pastry cream)

4 egg yolks

100g (3½oz) caster sugar

30g (1¼oz) plain flour

1 vanilla pod, with a line scored down the side, or ½ tsp vanilla extract

350ml (12fl oz) milk

100ml (3½fl oz) double or regular cream

Grated zest of 1 orange

Cont. overleaf

For the choux pastry, please see method on page 54.

Preheat the oven to 220°C (425°F), Gas mark 7.

Line a baking tray with baking parchment. Put the choux pastry into the piping bag fitted with the large nozzle and pipe the dough into twenty rounds about 4cm (1½in) in diameter, spaced about 4cm (1½in) apart on the tray to allow for expansion. Use a small wet knife to stop the dough coming out when you have finished piping each puff. If you don't have a piping bag, you can use two dessertspoons, scraping the dough off one with the other to make rounds of a similar size.

Brush the puffs gently with some of the remaining beaten egg and bake in the oven for 15–20 minutes or until they are puffed up, golden and crisp. Remove the puffs from the oven and, using a skewer or the tip of a small sharp knife, make a hole in the side or the base of each puff. Return to the oven and bake for a further 5 minutes to allow the steam to escape. Allow the puffs to cool on a wire rack.

For the crème pâtissière, in a bowl, whisk the egg yolks with the sugar until light and thick, then sift in the flour and stir to mix.

Place the vanilla pod, if using, in a saucepan with the milk and bring it slowly just up to the boil. Remove the vanilla pod and pour the milk onto the egg mixture, whisking all the time. Return the mixture to the pan and stir over a low to medium heat until it comes up to a gentle boil (it must boil for it to thicken). Continue to cook, stirring all the time (or use a whisk if it looks lumpy), for 2 minutes or until very thick.

For the caramel sauce

225g (8oz) caster or granulated sugar

110g (4oz) butter

175ml (6fl oz) double cream

Pinch of salt

Icing sugar, to dust

Equipment

Piping bag fitted with a large and small nozzle (optional)

Remove the saucepan from the heat, add the vanilla extract, if using, and pour into a bowl. If the mixture goes a little lumpy while cooking, remove the saucepan from the heat and whisk well. If it is still lumpy when cooked, push it through a sieve. Place in a bowl and allow to cool completely.

Pour the cream into a bowl, whisk until stiff, then fold into the cooled pastry cream with the orange zest. Use the piping bag with a small nozzle attached to pipe the orange cream into the choux puffs in the hole that you made while they were baking.

To make the caramel sauce, dissolve the sugar in 75ml (3fl oz) water in a pan over a medium heat. Stir in the butter, raise the heat a little, and bubble, stirring occasionally, for about 8–10 minutes until it turns a light toffee colour. Turn off the heat and stir in half the cream. When the bubbles die down, stir in the rest of the cream and a pinch of salt.

To finish, place the choux puffs on serving plates, dust with icing sugar, then pour over the warm caramel sauce to serve.

Rachel's Tips: The crème pâtissière can be frozen or maybe made a couple of days in advance and stored in the fridge before using.

The caramel sauce can be stored in the fridge for up to two weeks and reheated when necessary.

FESTIVE TREATS

Easter chocolate meringue cake

Sweet wine syllabub

Spiced plum tarte tatin

Festive fruity steamed pudding

Mulled port pears with port jelly

Negroni jelly with clementine sorbet

Iced pumpkin cake

Spiced cranberry, white chocolate and
orange biscotti

Nectarine and sloe gin jelly trifle

Eggnog crème brûlée

Chocolate and vanilla swirl biscuits

Cinnamon, apple and raisin pastries

This is a variation of a cake that my sister makes. It has an unusual method, where two layers of meringue and chocolate cake are baked together in the oven before being sandwiched together with whipped cream. The three different textures come together, resulting in a perfectly festive Easter treat. Feel free to put raspberries or sliced strawberries in with the cream, too.

Easter chocolate meringue cake

SERVES 8–10

For the cake

100g (3½oz) butter, softened, plus extra for greasing

350g (12oz) caster sugar

2 eggs

225g (8oz) plain flour

50g (2oz) cocoa powder

¾ tsp baking powder

¼ tsp bicarbonate of soda

Pinch of salt

225ml (8fl oz) buttermilk or sour milk

For the meringue

3 egg whites

150g (5oz) caster sugar

275ml (9½fl oz) double or regular cream

Icing sugar, for dusting

Equipment

2 x 23cm (9in) spring-form cake tins

Preheat the oven to 165°C (325°F), Gas mark 3. Brush the sides of the tins with melted or soft butter and dust with flour. Make sure the bases are upside down, so there is no lip and the cakes can slide off easily when cooked.

To make the cake, place the butter in a mixing bowl and beat until very soft. Add the sugar and one of the eggs and beat again, then add the other egg and mix. Sift the flour, cocoa powder, baking powder, bicarbonate of soda and salt into a separate bowl and set aside. Measure the buttermilk and set aside also.

Now, start the meringue. Place the egg whites in a bowl and whisk until frothy using an electric food mixer or hand-held electric beater. Add in half the sugar and continue whisking until the mixture holds stiff peaks. Turn off the whisk and fold in the remaining sugar.

Next, go back to the cake. Fold in the sifted dry ingredients and the buttermilk, then divide the mixture between the two cake tins, making sure they are level. Divide the meringue between the two cakes and spread out evenly over the cakes.

Cook in the oven for 1 hour or until a skewer inserted into the centre comes out clean. Take out of the oven and allow to sit in the tin for 15–20 minutes before loosening around the sides with a small, sharp knife, removing the cakes from the tins and allowing to cool completely, meringue side up.

When ready to assemble, whip the cream until it just holds stiff peaks, then place one of the cakes (save the best cake for the top) on a cake stand. Spread the whipped cream over the top, then sit the second cake on top of the cream. Dust with icing sugar and serve.

The classic syllabub, which dates back as far as the early 1500s, is something of a cloud-like mousse, but as it contains no egg, it's even lighter again. Described by the *Oxford English Dictionary* as, 'A drink or dish made by milk or cream curdled by the admixture of wine, cider or other acid, and often sweetened and flavoured,' it was apparently made by the milkmaid, who would milk a cow directly into a jug of cider. This particularly festive version uses sweet dessert wine for a wonderfully decadent treat.

Sweet wine syllabub

SERVES 6

300ml (½ pint) double or regular cream

50g (2oz) caster sugar

125ml (4½fl oz) white dessert wine

Whip the cream very softly – it should not even hold soft peaks. In a separate bowl, stir the sugar into the wine until it has dissolved, then gently fold into the cream.

Divide into six small glasses and chill for 2 hours to softly set.

Serve with shortbread biscuits and the rest of the bottle of dessert wine.

Plums have a rich and complex flavour that stands up to, and even embraces, spices very well. This is a gorgeous dessert, perfect at Christmas or New Year. Make sure you pack in as many plum halves as possible, as when cooked they'll have shrunk in size.

Spiced plum tarte tatin

SERVES 6

For the pastry

150g (5oz) plain flour

Pinch of salt

75g (3oz) butter

65g (2½oz) crème fraîche or sour cream

For the filling

175g (6oz) caster or granulated sugar

25g (1oz) butter

½ tbsp mixed spice

8 ripe plums, halved lengthways and stones removed

Equipment

24cm (9½oz) ovenproof frying pan

Preheat the oven to 200°C (400°F), Gas mark 6.

First, make the pastry. Place the flour, salt and butter in a food processor and whiz briefly. Add two-thirds of the crème fraîche or sour cream and continue to whiz. You might add a little more, but not too much as the mixture should be just moist enough to come together. If making by hand, rub the butter into the flour and salt until it resembles coarse breadcrumbs then, using your hands, add just enough crème fraîche or sour cream to bring it together.

With your hands, flatten out the ball of dough until it is about 2cm (¾in) thick, then wrap in cling film or place in a plastic bag and leave in the fridge for at least 30 minutes.

Place the sugar, butter and mixed spice together in the ovenproof frying pan. Stir together and boil, uncovered, for 5–8 minutes, until the mixture turns into a golden brown caramel. Place the plums cut side down in the pan of syrupy caramel. Cook for 3 minutes, then remove from the heat.

Roll out the pastry to the same size as the inside diameter of the pan and place it on the plums, tucking it into the edges. Bake it in the oven for 20–25 minutes or until golden brown on top. Take out of the oven and allow to sit for 1 minute before placing a plate over the top and carefully flipping it over, holding tightly.

Serve in slices with softly whipped cream.

A very jolly Christmas pudding; this one is seriously citrussy with the addition of orange liqueur and lots of marmalade. Feel free to chop and change the dried fruit; dates or sultanas would work well, too.

Festive fruity steamed pudding

SERVES 6–8

For the fruit topping

100g (3½oz) orange marmalade

100ml (3½fl oz) orange liqueur, such as Cointreau, Grand Marnier or triple sec

50g (2oz) dried cranberries, roughly chopped

50g (2oz) dried apricots, chopped

For the pudding

200g (7oz) butter, plus extra for greasing

200g (7oz) caster sugar

3 eggs, lightly beaten

250g (9oz) plain flour

1 tsp mixed spice

½ tsp baking powder

¼ tsp bicarbonate of soda

75ml (3fl oz) buttermilk

Equipment

1.7 litre (3 pint) pudding basin and kitchen string

To start, place the marmalade, liqueur, cranberries and apricots in a small saucepan, bring to the boil and simmer for 2–3 minutes until the mixture becomes slightly stickier, then set aside to cool.

Next, make the pudding batter. Cream the butter in a large bowl or in an electric food mixer until soft. Add the sugar and beat until the mixture is light and fluffy. Gradually add the beaten eggs, beating well between each addition.

Sift in the flour, mixed spice, baking powder and bicarbonate of soda and mix into the batter until just incorporated. Next, add the buttermilk and mix together to make a dropping consistency.

Lightly butter the pudding basin. Pour the fruit mix into the base of the prepared pudding basin and spoon in the sponge batter.

Cut out a sheet of baking parchment at least 8cm (3in) larger than the top of the basin, fold a crease in the middle (this allows the paper to expand as the pudding cooks) and tie the sheet over the lip of the bowl with heatproof string.

Place the pudding in a saucepan not much larger than the basin and carefully pour in enough hot water to come three-quarters of the way up the basin. Cover and boil for approximately 1½ hours until a skewer inserted in the centre of the pudding comes out clean and it feels spongy to the touch. Keep the water topped up in the saucepan during cooking.

Carefully remove the basin from the pan and turn out onto a warmed serving plate, allowing the fruit to fall down the sides. Serve with lightly whipped cream.

I love how some old-fashioned cookery terms find their way into our everyday language today. One example of this is the phrase to 'mull things over', meaning to slowly think and consider an idea or thought. This is most likely derived from the very slow and deliberate process of infusing juices, brandies or wines with spices over a low heat.

In this recipe, pears are poached in a sweet port syrup infused with cardamom, cinnamon and star anise. The poaching liquid is then given another star turn and set with gelatine to make a truly festive feast.

Mulled port pears with port jelly

SERVES 6

225ml (8fl oz) port

225g (8oz) caster or granulated sugar

7 green cardamom pods, bashed

1 cinnamon stick

2 star anise

2 strips of orange rind (removed with a peeler)

6 pears, peeled

2 sheets of gelatine

Place the port, 225ml (8fl oz) water, the sugar, spices and orange rind in a saucepan that will just fit the pears. Place on a medium heat and stir until the sugar has dissolved. Place the pears neatly in the saucepan with the port syrup. Cover with a disc of baking parchment and a lid, then simmer for 20 minutes. Turn over the pears, then cook for a further 20–30 minutes until the pears are soft.

Remove the pears and strain the juices into a measuring jug. Add enough water to make up to 475ml (16fl oz). Pour 75ml (3fl oz) of this liquid back over the pears and keep aside in the saucepan, then set aside.

Place two sheets of gelatine in a bowl of cold water for 3–5 minutes to soften, then remove from the water and squeeze out any excess liquid. Add the softened gelatine sheets to the warm syrup, stirring to dissolve. If the syrup has cooled too much, the gelatine will not dissolve, in which case, heat the syrup again.

Divide the liquid into six small glasses or moulds lined with cling film and chill in the fridge for 3–4 hours until set.

To serve, warm the pears gently in the syrup, then turn out the jellies onto plates, place a warm pear on the side and drizzle over some of the syrup. Serve with softly whipped cream. These are just as delicious cold.

I was trying to work out how I could incorporate my favourite cocktail, the negroni, into this book. It was either going to be a sorbet or a jelly, but seeing as how a negroni is basically just alcohol, the chances of a negroni sorbet freezing properly weren't very high. So a negroni jelly it is, and it goes superbly with the clementine sorbet. Be warned, though: just the one will do, otherwise you'll be under, or on top of, the table.

Negroni jelly with clementine sorbet

MAKES 4

For the sorbet

Juice of ½ lemon

Juice and zest of 4 clementines, tangerines or satsumas

50g (2oz) caster or granulated sugar

For the jellies

45ml (1½fl oz) gin

45ml (1½fl oz) Campari

45ml (1½fl oz) Martini Rosso

1 sheet of gelatine

45ml (1½fl oz) orange juice

25g (1oz) caster or granulated sugar

Equipment

Ice-cream machine or sorbetière

To make the sorbet, mix together the lemon juice, clementine juice, zest and sugar, stirring to dissolve the sugar. Then freeze in an ice-cream maker according to the manufacturer's instructions.

To make the jellies, in a bowl mix together the gin, Campari and Martini. Soften a sheet of gelatine in cold water for 3–5 minutes, then squeeze out any excess liquid. Pour the orange juice into a saucepan, add the sugar and place on a low heat. Stir just until the sugar has dissolved, then remove from the heat.

Add the softened gelatine to the warm orange juice, then mix everything together well. Strain through a sieve into the alcohol mixture, then pour into four glasses or lightly greased moulds.

Place in the fridge to set for at least 3 hours, then turn out and serve with a scoop of the clementine sorbet.

Rachel's Tip: If you don't have an ice-cream machine, transfer the mixture to a freezerproof bowl and place in the freezer. After 30 minutes, remove from the freezer and run a spatula around the edge of the container, where ice crystals will have formed. Stir the sorbet like this every 30 minutes until all the juices have frozen.

A great recipe to make at Halloween time with the scooped-out pumpkin. This has the North American flavours that I adore: sugar and spice and all things nice.

Iced pumpkin cake

SERVES 8–10

425g (15oz) pumpkin, peeled, deseeded and cut into roughly 2cm (¾in) chunks (300g/11oz when prepared)

250g (9oz) plain flour

2 tsp baking powder

250g (9oz) caster sugar

¼ tsp ground cloves

½ tsp ground ginger

½ tsp ground nutmeg

½ tsp ground cinnamon

½ tsp salt

2 eggs

150g (5oz) butter, melted

For the icing

200g (7oz) icing sugar

2–3 tbsp orange juice

Equipment

23cm (9in) spring-form cake tin

Line the spring-form cake tin with baking parchment.

First, cook the pumpkin. Place in a saucepan with 200ml (7fl oz) water, bring to a simmer and cook for 20–25 minutes until tender. Allow to cool, then mash well or whiz in a food processor to form a pulp.

Preheat the oven to 180°C (350°F), Gas mark 4.

In a bowl, sift the flour together with the baking powder, then mix in the rest of the dry ingredients. In a separate bowl, thoroughly mix together the eggs, butter and pumpkin. Combine with the dry ingredients and place in the cake tin.

Bake for 45 minutes until a skewer inserted into the centre of the cake comes out clean. Remove from the oven and place on a wire rack to cool for 10 minutes before turning out of the tin.

As the cake cools, make the icing. Place the sugar in a bowl and mix in just enough orange juice to make a spreadable icing, making sure it's not too wet. If there's too much orange juice, the icing will fall off the sides of the cake, but if there's not enough, it will be difficult to spread.

For the icing, I like to use a palette knife that I regularly dip into a jug of boiling water, as this helps to spread it out. So, using the palette knife, spread the icing over the top of the cake. Allow the icing to set (this takes about 15 minutes), then cut into slices to serve.

This cake keeps well for a week (the pumpkin seems to prevent it from drying out).

While these are a very welcome treat to have in a jar over Christmas, they're actually delicious any time of the year. I adore the white chocolate, orange and dried cranberry trio, but other dried fruit and chocolate also work well.

Spiced cranberry, white chocolate and orange biscotti

MAKES ABOUT 40 BISCOTTI

100g (3½oz) plain flour, plus extra for dusting

100g (3½oz) caster sugar

1 tsp baking powder

½ tsp ground cinnamon

½ tsp ground nutmeg

80g (3oz) white chocolate, chopped

50g (2oz) dried cranberries, roughly chopped

50g (2oz) candied orange peel, roughly chopped

1 egg, beaten

Preheat the oven to 160°C (320°F), Gas mark 3.

Sift together the flour, sugar, baking powder and spices into a large bowl. Add the chocolate, cranberries and candied orange and mix well, then mix in the beaten egg to form a soft dough. Flour your hands, then turn the dough out onto a lightly floured work surface and form into a sausage about 30cm (12in) long and 3cm (1¼in) in diameter.

Place on a baking tray and bake for about 25 minutes until browned and just set, then remove and allow to cool on a wire rack for 5 minutes.

Cut into slices about 5mm (¼in) thick, then lay flat on the tray and bake for a further 10 minutes.

Turn all the biscotti over on the tray, return to the oven and continue to bake for 10 minutes more. They should be a light golden colour on both cut sides. Cool on a wire rack, then transfer to an airtight container where they will keep for up to two weeks.

258 · FESTIVE TREATS

A very grown-up trifle. Sloe gin is a quintessential Christmas ingredient as, if you've made it yourself, you'll know that happily it matures perfectly by mid-December. The nectarines, while not a seasonal local fruit where I live, are a little festive treat to make this trifle truly delicious.

Nectarine and sloe gin jelly trifle

SERVES 8

For the jelly

100g (3½oz) caster sugar

75ml (3fl oz) sloe gin or grenadine

Juice of ½ lemon

2 sheets of gelatine

400g (14oz) nectarines

For the sponge

50g (2oz) caster sugar

50g (2oz) butter

1 egg, beaten

50g (2oz) plain flour

½ tsp baking powder

Cont. opposite

To make the jelly, place the sugar and 150ml (5fl oz) water in a saucepan on a high heat, stir and simmer for just 2 minutes to dissolve the sugar. Remove from the heat, stir in the sloe gin and lemon juice and set aside. At this stage, remove 5 tablespoons of syrup and keep to drizzle over the sponge.

Next, place the gelatine in a bowl and cover with cold water, then let stand for 3–5 minutes to soften. Remove the gelatine from the water and squeeze out any excess liquid, then add the softened gelatine to the warm syrup and stir to dissolve. If the syrup has cooled, gently reheat.

Slice the nectarines thinly and add to the syrup. Divide evenly among eight glasses, filling them not more than halfway, then place in the fridge to set. This should take 3–4 hours.

Preheat the oven to 160°C (320°F), Gas mark 3.

To make the sponge, place the sugar and butter in a bowl and use a wooden spoon or the paddle attachment of an electric food mixer to cream together until light and fluffy. Add the beaten egg and mix in, then sift in the flour and baking powder, folding together just until combined.

Divide the batter into four paper bun cases in the bun tray, then place in the oven and bake for 15–20 minutes until risen and springy to the touch. Remove from the oven and place on a wire rack to cool then, when cool, slice each bun in half horizontally.

For the custard

150ml (5fl oz) single, whipping or regular cream

4 strips of orange rind (removed with a peeler)

150ml (5fl oz) milk

2 egg yolks

25g (1oz) caster or granulated sugar

Equipment

6-hole bun tray (smaller than a cupcake or muffin tray)

To make the custard, place the cream, orange rind and milk in a small saucepan and place on a medium heat. Bring up to just before the boil, then remove from the heat. In a bowl, whisk together the egg yolks and sugar. Pour the hot creamy milk over the sugar and egg yolks and whisk together. Return to the saucepan, discarding the orange strips, then cook on a low heat, stirring constantly until the mixture starts to thicken. Be careful that it doesn't get too hot or else you will have sweet scrambled eggs. Transfer the custard to a bowl to cool slightly.

To assemble the trifles, remove the jellies from the fridge, place a disc of sponge on top of each one and drizzle a spoon of the retained syrup over each sponge disc. Divide the custard out evenly to cover each disc of sponge and return it to the fridge to allow the custard to set.

To serve, add a good spoonful of softly whipped cream on top of each trifle and decorate with a mint or sweet geranium leaf if you wish.

Rachel's Tips: Replace the sloe gin with orange juice for an alcohol-free version. Raspberries also work really well in place of the nectarines. This recipe can be doubled or tripled to make one large trifle.

A centuries-old drink recipe containing eggs, alcohol and cream, eggnog was often used in toasts to good health and prosperity. It's long been associated with Christmas and is especially festive when turned into a celebratory crème brûlée.

Eggnog crème brûlée

SERVES 4

2 egg yolks

1 tbsp caster or granulated sugar

240ml (8fl oz) double or regular cream

60ml (2½fl oz) brandy

½ cinnamon stick

½ vanilla pod, split and scraped

For the caramel topping

110g (4oz) caster sugar

Ideally, make the custard the day before the crème brûlée is needed, or at least 8 hours beforehand. Mix the egg yolks together with the sugar. Place the cream, brandy, cinnamon and vanilla pod in a saucepan. Place on a medium heat and warm just until 'shivering', but do not boil.

When hot, remove the cinnamon and vanilla pod (these can be rinsed, dried and used again) and pour the cream slowly over the egg yolks, whisking all the time. Return to the saucepan and cook on a low heat, stirring constantly, just until it is thick enough to coat the back of a spoon. It must not boil or the egg yolks will scramble. Pour into four cups, glasses or ramekins. Allow to cool, then place in the fridge to chill overnight. Be careful not to break the skin that forms.

The following day, or 8 hours later, make the caramel topping. Dissolve the sugar for the caramel topping in 75ml (3fl oz) water. Place in a saucepan and on a medium–high heat. Bring to the boil and cook until the sugar caramelises and turns a chestnut-brown colour. Do not stir while it is boiling or the sugar will crystallise, though you can swirl the pan when it starts to brown a little at the edges. Remove from the heat and immediately spoon a thin layer of caramel over the top of the custards, making sure not to 'swirl' them to help spread the caramel. Doing this can break the skin on top of the custard, which will cause the caramel to sink.

Allow to cool and set for at least 15 minutes, then serve. The crème brûlées will sit in a dry atmosphere for 2–3 hours.

Rachel's Tip: If you have a blowtorch, instead of making caramel, scatter over the custards a 2mm (⅛in) layer of caster or granulated sugar. Wave the blowtorch slowly over the sugar, from about 10cm (4in) away, until it is deep golden and caramelised. Allow to sit for 5 minutes before serving.

I like the *Charlie and the Chocolate Factory*-esque look of these. A delicious swirl made up of two of the best-suited flavours in baking: chocolate and vanilla. You can cook a few or all of these biscuits at one time.

Chocolate and vanilla swirl biscuits

MAKES ABOUT 36 BISCUITS

150g (5oz) butter, softened

110g (4oz) caster sugar

1 egg

Icing sugar, for dusting

For the vanilla swirl

2 tsp vanilla extract

150g (5oz) plain flour

¼ tsp baking powder

For the chocolate swirl

35g (1¼oz) cocoa powder

115g (4oz) plain flour

¼ tsp baking powder

Preheat the oven to 180°C (350°F), Gas mark 4. Line a baking tray with baking parchment.

Cream the butter with the sugar and beat until it is light and fluffy, then beat in the egg. At this point, divide the mixture evenly between two bowls. There should be about 160g (5½oz) mixture in each. Into the vanilla swirl bowl, add the vanilla extract, then sift in the flour and baking powder and mix to a soft dough. Into the chocolate swirl bowl, sift the cocoa powder, flour and baking powder. Mix this to a soft dough as well.

Dust two sheets of baking parchment with icing sugar (make sure you use enough, so that the dough doesn't stick). Roll out each ball of dough on a different sheet of parchment, dusting the top with icing sugar too, to a rectangle of 20 x 30cm (8 x 12in). Both rectangles need to be the same size.

Slide one onto the other layer evenly and, starting from the long 30cm (12in) end, roll tightly into a swirled log. Be careful, as the dough is quite fragile. Wrap in the paper and place in the fridge to chill for at least 15 minutes (they can sit in the fridge for up to two weeks).

Cut into slices about 7.5mm (¼in) thick. Bake for 15 minutes until the underside is golden on the outside and just dry to the touch. Transfer carefully to a wire rack to cool.

Rachel's Tip: The log will keep in the fridge for two weeks. Simply cut and cook as many swirls as you need.

Another gorgeous way to use puff pastry. These are deliciously moreish, sweet and spicy, and just perfect with a cup of coffee.

Cinnamon, apple and raisin pastries

MAKES 6 PASTRIES

3 small eating apples, peeled, cored and cut into 1cm (½in) chunks

100g (3½oz) caster or granulated sugar

40g (1½oz) raisins

½ tsp ground ginger

1 tsp ground cinnamon

250g (9oz) puff pastry

1 egg, beaten

3 tsp demerara sugar

Preheat the oven to 220°C (425°F), Gas mark 7. Line a baking tray with baking parchment.

First, prepare the spiced apple filling. Place the apples in a saucepan with the sugar, raisins, spices and 3 tablespoons water. Cover and cook for about 10 minutes until the apples are soft. Take the lid off and cook, uncovered, for another 1–2 minutes until there's no liquid left in the pan. Tip the mixture onto a plate and allow to cool.

Roll the pastry into a rectangle about 35 x 25cm (14 x 10in). The pastry should be about 3mm (⅛in) thick. Trim the edges of the pastry (not too much, as this will be discarded) and cut the pastry into six squares.

Divide the spiced apple mixture among the six squares, placing it in the centre of the squares. With each one, fold in each of the four corners so that they almost meet in the middle. Brush the tops with beaten egg, then sprinkle with demerara sugar.

Lift the pastries carefully onto the prepared tray and bake for 10–12 minutes until golden and crisp. Allow to cool slightly before eating.

Index

Acknowledgements

It is with a mixture of emotions that I write the acknowledgements, as this is the final and last chapter of the book. One half of me is sighing with relief that I've got this far and somehow managed not to lose all my recipes in that cloud up there, while the other half of me is almost sad, as it's like saying goodbye to a friend. And in this case it's a really lovely, sweet friend.

As is always the case, there were many people involved in making this book come to fruition. At HarperCollins, where the project turned from an idea into delicious reality, I was lucky enough to work with Georgina Mackenzie, Martin Topping, James Empringham, Carole Tonkinson, Virginia Woolstencroft, Hannah Gammon.

A huge thank you to photographer Tara Fisher and also to Mario Sierra, Joss Herd, Jordan Bourke, Rachel Webb, Kathryn Morrissey, Tabitha Hawkins and Liz MacCarthy for doing stunningly stellar work on the shoot for the book.

A huge hug and sincere thanks to Ivan Whelan for the enormous contribution he made to this book and all his help testing the recipes with me.

While the final editing for this book was taking place I was also working on filming the *All Things Sweet* television series. David Nottage of Liverpool Street Productions, Karen Gilchrist, Michael Connock, Annabel Hornsby, Rob Partis, Sam Jackson, Ed Beck, Ivan Whelan, Jette Vindi, Gail O'Driscoll, Rebecca Bullen, Al Blaine, Scott Breckenridge, Duncan Hart, Ewan Henesy, Richard Hobbs: you are all incredible at what you do and somehow managed to make our relentless shoot schedule not only painless, but really good fun, too!

A big thanks also to everyone at Ballymaloe House and Cookery School, Fiona Lindsay and all at Limelight Management, Ardmore Pottery, Article, and Eden (two beautiful homeware shops in Dublin), Nougat, sphere One by Lucy Downes (for the divine cashmere), JR Ryall, Diarmaid Falvey, Conor Pyne, Brian Walsh of RTE , my wonderful parents Brian and Hallfridur O'Neill, my also wonderful parents-in-law Tim and Darina Allen, and my super-fabulous sister and brother-in-law Simone and Dodo Michel.

Isaac, thank you for everything. You make everything run smoothly at home and in work, you think outside the box (which I don't), you're the most wonderful cook, and most importantly you are my gorgeous and lovely husband.

I dedicate this book to my children and godchildren who are, without doubt All Things Sweet: Josh, Lucca and Scarlett Allen, Lola and Rosa Michel, Matilda Cuddigan-Eck, James Whyld and Sophie Gleeson.